THE
OLD SHIP
A Prospect of Brighton

By the same author:

Raffles: the Story of Singapore
The Palace: a Profile of St Moritz
Chianti: the Land, the People, and the Wine
Chianti: Storia e Cultura
Napoleon to Nasser: the Story of Modern Egypt
The History of Skiing & Other Winter Sports
Motor Sports, an Illustrated History
Year of the Tiger

With Michael Wynn Jones:

Lloyd's of London, an Illustrated History
A Hundred Years of Motoring, a RAC Social History of the Car

Editor, with René Burri and H.V. Morton:

In Search of the Holy Land

THE
OLD SHIP
A Prospect of Brighton

Raymond Flower

CROOM HELM

London · Sydney · Dover, New Hampshire

For Joyce, Vivienne and Estelle

© 1986 Raymond Flower
Picture research and captions by Judy Middleton
Croom Helm Ltd, Provident House, Burrell Row, Beckenham, Kent BR3 1AT
Croom Helm Australia Pty Ltd, Suite 4, 6th Floor, 64–76 Kippax Street,
Surry Hills, NSW 2010, Australia

British Library Cataloguing in Publication Data

Flower, Raymond
   The old ship: a prospect of Brighton.
   1. Brighton (East Sussex)—History
   I. Title
   942.2'56   DA690.B78

ISBN 0–7099–1077–0

Croom Helm, 51 Washington Street, Dover,
New Hampshire 03820, USA

Library of Congress Cataloguing in Publication Data

Flower, Raymond, 1921–
   The Old Ship: a prospect of Brighton.

   1. Old Ship Hotel (Brighton, East Sussex)
   2. Brighton (East Sussex)—Social life and customs.
   I. Title.
   TX941.048F48   1986   942.2'56   86–4544
ISBN 0–7099–1077–0

Printed and bound in Great Britain at the University Press in the city of Oxford

Contents

List of Colour Plates

1. Portrait of Charles II
2. Portrait of Nicholas Tettersell
3. The *Royal Escape* after van de Velde
4. Lambert's View of Brighthelmston in 1765
5. Portrait of the Prince of Wales by van der Puyl
6. The Barrymore brothers
7. The Court at Brighton à la Chinese
8. The Great Joss and his Playthings
9. By Royal Authority—a new way of mounting a horse
10. The Royal Pavilion from the Steine
11. Great chandelier in the Banqueting Room
12. Roof of the port-cochère
13. Royal Pavilion under snow
14. Pavilion Gardens in Spring
15. The Chain Pier
16. St Nicolas's Church
17. Brighton Hurdle Race, 1833
18. Two Bathing Beauties
19. Lewes Crescent
20. The West Pier, illustrated on cover of the 'Brighton Quadrilles'
21. The Palace Pier at sunset
22. Motor Rally outside the Old Ship in 1908
23. Rex Whistler's painting *The Spirit of Brighton*
24. Rottingdean windmill
25. Modern-day beach scene
26. Marina
27. Lanes
28. Horse Driving Trials, Stanmer Park, 1984
29. The bombed Grand Hotel, October 1984

List of Black and White Illustrations

Picture Credits

Colour illustrations

Norman Browne: 11, 13, 14, 19, 21, 24, 25, 26, 28, 29, 30
Bob Curtis: 27
East Sussex County Library: 10, 15, 16, 18, 20, 22
Hove Museum: 4, 5, 17
Old Ship Hotel: 1, 2, 3
Royal Pavilion, Art Gallery and Museums, Brighton: 6, 7, 8, 9, 12, 23

Black and white illustrations

Brighton Gazette: 102
East Sussex County Library: 1, 3, 5, 7, 8, 10, 11, 12, 14, 15, 17, 18, 20, 21, 22,
    23, 24, 25, 27, 28, 29, 30, 31, 32, 35, 36, 37, 38, 39, 40, 41, 42, 45, 46, 47,
    48, 50, 51, 52, 54, 55, 56, 57, 58, 59, 60, 62, 63, 64, 65, 66, 67, 69, 70, 72,
    73, 77, 78, 81, 82, 84, 85, 89, 90, 91, 92, 93, 94, 95, 96, 97, 98, 99, 100,
    101, 106
Evening Argus: 104, 105, 110
Epoque: 107
Hove Museum: 6, 9, 68
Howlett & Clarke, Brighton: 16
National Portrait Gallery: 13, 19
Old Ship Hotel: 103, 108, 109
Royal College of Music: 26
Royal Pavilion, Art Gallery and Museums, Brighton: 2, 4, 61

Major John Bacon: 33, 34, 43, 44, 71, 83
Philippe Garner: 53
James S. Gray: 74, 80
Robert Jeeves: 76
Judy Middleton: 49, 79, 86, 87, 88
Peter Quantrill: 75

Front cover photograph by Norman Browne

Portraits on page 113 by Trish Burgess

Prologue

Should one return to one's childhood haunts? After all, people vanish, buildings are transformed, the landscape changes, and the time-scale itself begins to nag when you revisit a place where you once raced up and down the hills and thought nothing of playing ten sets of tennis at a go . . .

For a while I sat ruminating as the sunlight flickered along the brindled waves of our wake and the familiar chalk-coloured cliffs came into view. Framed by the plate-glass windows of the cross-channel ferry, they seemed for an instant like something out of Norse fable—mysterious, romantic. But then the ship turned sharply to point her prow at Dover harbour. Time to stop woolgathering and go down to the car.

Soon we were driving along the trim little esplanade, keeping carefully to the left and dithering at the roundabouts as one does in those first few unfocused moments. At Folkestone the rain started coming down like stair-rods, so we pressed on to Hythe before making a dash into the nearest pub. Engulfed in the geniality of dark beams and chatter, I downed a welcoming pint of bitter and ordered fried plaice for lunch. 'Trust you to have fish and chips the moment you arrive' laughed M, who was tucking into bangers and mash herself. Yes, it was good to be back again. For though so much in England has changed, even more has remained invincibly the same, its old pleasures and astonishments intact. The adventure was beginning!

It had started a few days previously at the Frankfurt Book Fair, to whose sacramental dazzle I am drawn each October by what can only be some atavistic spell. What else would impel a writer to that monstrous emporium where half a million new books are exposed like cans of dog food in a giant supermarket? Yet this act of self-immolation can have its reward. For over dinner in a Rhineside restaurant, inspired perhaps by fresh salmon-trout and hock from the vineyards outside, my publishers had conjured up the notion of a book about Brighton.

A splendid suggestion! Brighton, with its brag and its elegance, its opportunism and its variety: a cocotte if not a queen of resorts, scribbled with the signatures of princes and posturers . . . Of course I jumped at the idea. It was there, after all, that I had been weaned, so to speak; for while my parents gyrated abroad I was sent, as a tearful eight-year-old, to a preparatory school in Hove. (Mowden still thrives, I am glad to say, unlike some of its rivals.) And during the holidays I was farmed out on relatives—uncle Ernest Oulton, who ran the Sussex Eye hospital, was something of a local figure in his day: an international Rugger cap, member of the Alpine Club, and Cambridge Tennis Blue who still took to the court at the age of 75. In his cheerful household Christmas was an exuberant time, full of children's parties and beagling on the Downs; later, when I moved on to public school, there were skating sessions at the ice-stadium, evenings at the Theatre Royal and black-tie dinners at the Old Ship, where my uncle's favourite trick was to produce a magnifying glass and search for maggots in the Stilton . . .

Now, after so many years absence, I was heading back to Brighton. And if our immediate destination was the Old Ship Hotel, this was not merely because the owners are old friends who had sportingly offered to help me with the project. Paramount in my mind was the thought that the Old Ship is Brighton's oldest hostelry—its most ancient secular institution, I believe. For centuries the Old Ship has been the centre of local activities, and to have a focal point such as this is a godsend when one starts peering back over the long, glittering prospect of events. Its elegant bow windows, through which so many generations have watched the animated scene, would make an admirable vantage-point, I felt, for getting to grips with the place: to intuit how Brighton grew its own history, its own temperament, and its own quite distinguishing personality. Today the Old Ship may seem to be just one of many other swanky hotels on the sea-front. Granted, but within its ancient fabric are hidden intimations of a rumbustious past if one is attentive enough to tune into them.

Meanwhile the countryside looked lovely once the rain had stopped, and we sped through those delectable towns that stud the south coast like jewelled pendants—Winchelsea and Rye, Hastings and St Leonards, Eastbourne—all polished and prinked and so infinitely more attractive than their opposite numbers on the Norman shore. This, surely, is the right way to approach Brighton: a delightful overture followed, as it were, by a 'commercial' between Newhaven and Roedean (so aloof and unbending—was ever a scented hankerchief dropped on its stairs?) to herald the palatial sweep of Kemp Town and the first thrilling vista of those white crescents, those Georgian squares.

When we parked in front of the Old Ship and went into the panelled foyer, it was like being introduced into a microcosm of history: elegant Adamesque drawing-rooms on one side, a thick-carpeted modern bar on the other. John Bacon, whose family owned the place for a century and a quarter, was there to welcome us. 'Meet you for a drink at Tettersell's' he said, as the bags went upstairs.

'Tettersell's?' echoed M, perhaps with horses in mind.

'We like to think of Nick Tettersell as being our founding father,' explained Major Bacon. 'After all, it was he who saved Charles II in 1651.'

And that seems as good a point as any at which to begin our story.

CHAPTER 1

The Royal Escape

From the moment he saw the disposition of Cromwell's forces from Worcester Cathedral tower on that misty autumn morning, it must have been clear to Charles Stuart that the battle was lost. Yet so well did his Highlanders fight when he led them out of Sidbury Gate, so pugnaciously did they press forward, that initially the Ironsides were repulsed. At this point, a cavalry charge might very well have carried the day. But, alas, no Scottish horse went galloping off to back up the infantry. As General Leslie had so often warned, they had little stomach for a fight on foreign soil. Instead, they remained motionless in the rear, while the foot-soldiers, their ammunition expended, struggled with halberds and the butt-ends of their muskets until they were overwhelmed by sheer weight of numbers.

Suddenly it became a question of saving the King. Charles was still trying to rally the cavalry when Lord Talbot seized the bridle of his big grey horse and almost manhandled him away. 'Let the King place himself among my men,' came Leslie's voice above the din, 'I will make sure that he gets back safely to Scotland.'

An officer raced up to report that the Roundheads were pouring into the town; cruelly outnumbered, the Royalists were being driven from Castle Hill. There was no time to lose. Halting at the gabled house on the corner of the Cornmarket which served as his headquarters only long enough to throw his papers on the fire, Charles rode off through St Martin's Gate with a handful of followers.

When the little party caught up with Leslie a mile beyond the town, the general again urged an immediate retreat into Scotland. By a forced march, he thought, they might be able to reach the border before Cromwell caught up with them. It certainly seemed the best thing to do. But the young king, taller by half a head than any of the others, refused point-blank. 'I will not go back to Scotland,' he announced. 'My mind is made up. I will go to London.'

No doubt he was thinking of the indignities he had suffered at the hands of the Covenanters. But his decision provoked a buzz of dissent. Only Lord Wilmot agreed with him. 'I will go with you, Sire,' he declared. 'In London they will never think of looking for you. And in London you have plenty of faithful friends who will get you back to France.'

So began the curious, picaresque episode in which an outlawed King of England was hounded through the woods and lanes of his own kingdom. Yet, as things turned out, the decision was wise. For whereas Leslie was captured, Charles eventually contrived to escape across the Channel. The astonishing thing is how, a fugitive with a huge price on his head, he managed to elude his pursuers for over six weeks.

Gone, of course, were the trappings of monarchy, the Garter riband, the jewelled George and the rings. Dressed in a coarse linen shirt, old green breeches, a leather doublet with pewter buttons, a greasy steeple-crowned hat and a pair of clumsy shoes that chafed his feet unmercifully, his hair cut short in the country fashion, his face and hands blackened with walnut and soot, Charles set out on his extraordinary adventure with only Lord Wilmot to accompany him.

He passed himself off as a Puritan by name of Will Jackson. A far cry from the popular image of Charles II as unbuttoned monarch with flowing locks and a well-stocked seraglio of 13 mistresses! Everyone knows how in the course of his wanderings from Shropshire to Dorset and through Hampshire to Sussex, he was forced to hide in an oak tree while the enemy searched below; to cram his huge frame into a tiny priest's hole for a whole night long; to disguise himself as an old woman, as a gipsy, as a gentleman's servant (who did not know how to turn a spit when told to do so). Yet one thing the 21-year-old King could not conceal was his height. For unlike his under-sized father, Charles was a gawky giant whose heavy sallow features and projecting underlip were all too well known. Several times he was recognised, fortunately by loyal subjects; often he narrowly escaped recognition and arrest. In a tavern at Bridport, for instance, a group of militiamen looked him straight in the face and remarked that he was very much like the description of the wanted king, and hardly had he slipped away from them than a troop of soldiers galloped into the town yelling whether anyone had seen 'a tall black fellow above two yards high with his hair cut short?'

Later, after the Restoration, Charles dictated the story of his adventures to Samuel Pepys, and his narrative was borne out by the accounts of various people who were involved—loyal characters such as Colonel Gounter of Racton, near Chichester, whose help Wilmot sought to find a boat that would carry the King to France. And since it is with the climax that we are concerned, that is, Charles' actual escape from Brighton, let us take up the narrative at this juncture.

Confessing a total ignorance of maritime affairs, though he lived only three miles from the sea, Gounter thought it best to approach Francis Mansell, a Chichester merchant who traded with France. Mansell was told that a passage was required for a friend of the colonel's who had to fly the country as a result of a duel. On being offered £50 for his services (in those days a substantial sum), he put the Colonel in touch with a certain 'Captain Nicholas Tettersell of Brighthelmstone', the owner of a little coal-brig called the *Surprise*, which was lying half-laden off Shoreham.

Tettersell, a thick-set man with a weather-beaten complexion and a voice loud enough to be heard above any gale, met Gounter and Mansell at Chichester. After much haggling it was agreed that he would carry the mythical duellists to France for the sum of £60 to be paid before they came aboard. For secrecy's sake, the little ship was to be moved from Shoreham to a quiet creek of the river Aduri, and while Mansell stayed behind to keep an eye on the captain, Gounter rode off to fetch the King from his hiding-place at Heale House, near Southampton.

The journey to Brighthelmstone had some anxious moments. As far as possible, the little party kept to trackways over the Downs through Hampshire and West Sussex to avoid being seen. But as they came abreast of the steep hill leading down into Arundel there was the noise of baying hounds and a moment later a company of horsemen came riding at full speed towards them.

'In amongst the trees, and dismount,' snapped Colonel Gounter, and by the time the hunt swept past they were out of sight, gripping their horses above the nostrils to prevent them from neighing. The huntsmen galloped on over the hill, obviously too absorbed in the chase to wonder at their sudden disappearance—which was just as well, for the party was headed by Captain Morley, the Governor of the Castle and as 'rabid a schismatic', muttered Gounter, as could be found in the whole of England. 'Was he indeed?' laughed the King, 'I can't say I fancied those starched mustachios of his!'

Crossing the Arun by Houghton Bridge, they went on towards Bramber, only to find the village was crowded with soldiers back from guard duties. Though Wilmot was all for turning back, the others kept their wits. 'It is not the first time I have ridden through a troop of Roundheads,' remarked Charles as they went on down the slight hill. Outside the alehouse there was hardly room for a horseman to pass; but Gounter pushed ahead with goodhumoured authority and with a few bawdy jokes brought the King safely through.

Yet hardly were they out of the village when there was the sound of hooves, and the Colonel, glancing over his shoulder, saw a troop of 30 or 40 militiamen bearing purposefully down on them. 'Slacken, Sire, slacken,' he urged the King, 'And for God's sake keep your hand away from your sword-hilt.'

'Swords won't help me, Harry, but wits may,' replied Charles, letting his reins go slack, as if he were ambling at his leisure. In a moment the troop thrust roughly past, nearly unseating the riders and spattering them with mud, but otherwise ignoring them. 'Well!' gasped the King, patting his mount as they disappeared around the corner, 'I think those were the worst few moments of any I have endured so far!'

Now Wilmot had had enough. 'We must get away from this road,' he said urgently, 'At any moment that troop may return, and take a closer look at your Majesty.' Sussex, he knew, was far from being a safe place, for although some of the gentry supported the Royalist cause, most of the ordinary Sussex folk were firmly on the Parliamentarian side. After all, five of the regicides who had signed Charles I's death warrant were Sussex men, and two had connections with Brighthelmstone: William Goffe's father had been Rector of Stanmer, Anthony Stapley owned a 250 acre estate in Hove and Preston. Wilmot refused, therefore, to let the King stay at Beeding, although arrangements had already been made; and according to Gounter's account 'for feare of the soldiers . . . carried the King out of the roade I know not whither. So we parted; they went where they thought safest.'

Once the party had split up, Gounter rode on into Brighthelmstone to check the final plans, while Wilmot took the King to Ovingdean Grange—which seems at that time to have belonged to Francis Mansell. Yet though Harrison Ainsworth's well-known novel revolves around his visit, Charles can only have stayed at Ovingdean for a matter of hours and certainly not days, for later in the evening of 14 October 1651 he arrived with Wilmot at the Olde George in Brighthelmstone.

Finding the town empty of soldiers, Gounter had engaged the best rooms at the George inn, and the royal party was joined there by Mansell and Tettersell. By unlucky chance, both Gaius Smith, the landlord, who had been a member of Charles I's bodyguard, and Captain Tettersell recognised the identity of the shabby Will Jackson. Beckoning the others on one side, the mariner complained that he had not been told the truth.

'He is the King, I know him very well, for he took my ship, together with other fishing vessels at Brighthelmstone, in the year 1648,' Tettersell insisted, omitting to add that the King had let him go again. While for his part, as soon as they were alone the innkeeper seized the tall young man's hand and kissed it, crying: 'God bless you wheresoever you go! I do not doubt before I die, but to be a lord and my wife a lady.' Charles laughed, though he realised that with a price of £1000 on his head things could turn out awkwardly—as Tettersell did not fail to remind Mansell.

For all this, the ship's captain protested his loyalty, declaring sententiously: 'I think I do God and my country good service in preserving the King, and by the grace of God I will venture my life and all for him, and set him safely on shore if I can, in France.' However, his loyalty did not prevent him from demanding better terms, which after some discussion were agreed.

Understandably the King's companions were reluctant to let Tettersell out of sight. Apart from the danger of betrayal, their hopes had already been thwarted a fortnight earlier when a boatman at Charmouth had been locked up by his wife, who feared the consequences of helping the fugitive monarch. But despite their misgivings, it was necessary for Tettersell to go off and collect the crew, along with a bottle of spirits and a clean shirt (which convinced *his* wife that he was up to no good). Meanwhile the King and Lord Wilmot slumbered in their clothes. At 2 a.m. they were aroused by the figure of Colonel Gounter silently pointing at his timepiece, and a few moments later the little party set out on horseback through the deserted alleys and along the beach to the creek where the *Surprise* lay aground.

Farewells were said. Charles and Wilmot clambered aboard up a ladder and secreted themselves in the tiny cabin, until at seven o'clock the incoming tide lifted the barque off the mud. Slowly she set sail in a westerly direction, for Poole was her usual destination, and Tettersell was anxious to avoid arousing any suspicions on shore.

There was virtually no wind, and throughout the morning and afternoon the little craft lay almost becalmed in the Channel, anxiously watched by Colonel Gounter who was on tenterhooks lest she should be forced ashore at the last moment. Then suddenly, almost at dusk, he saw her alter course. Just as her sails dipped over the horizon a party of red-coated militia reached Brighthelmstone searching for a 'tall black man, 6 feet 4 inches in height'. Soon everyone had learnt of the Royal Escape, and Brighthelmstone had made its bow into the country's history books.

CHAPTER 2

After the Restoration

1. Budgen's map of 1788 showing the Old Ship Tavern literally at the centre of Old Brighton

As Charles sat on deck in mid-channel, contentedly smoking his pipe, Tettersell ticked off one of the crew for staring at their passenger. 'Surely,' came the gruff response, 'A cat may look at a king?' It was this man, a Quaker named Thomas Carver, who carried him ashore through the waves at Fécamp.

The King had no further trouble reaching his family in Paris, though nine years of impoverished exile lay ahead before he was called back to the throne. By that time both Colonel Gounter and Lord Wilmot had died, but in his offhand way, Charles II did what he could for those who had helped him to escape. The Colonel's widow was given a pension, and Charles wrote personally to the headmaster of Winchester asking that her son should be admitted as a scholar. Wilmot's son, by now the Earl of Rochester, became notorious as a court favourite (and of course for his poems); it is no secret that he ended up badly. Francis Mansell, whose business had been ruined through suspicion of complicity in the royal flight, also received a pension—though for some reason it was not paid, causing Pepys to reflect on 'how mean a thing a King is'. But Carver had rather more luck. His only request was that the fellow Quakers who had been imprisoned for their religious beliefs should be released. Complaining that they were troublemakers, Charles promised Carver to free any six of them that he cared to name. Upon which the sailor retorted indignantly: 'What! Six poor Quakers for a king's ransom?', a reply that tickled the King so much that no less than 471 Quakers—among them John Bunyan, who had written the *Pilgrim's Progress* in Bedford Jail—were in the end set free.

Characteristically too, Nicholas Tettersell made sure that his part in the escapade was not overlooked. Immediately after the Restoration he draped his little barque from stem to stern with bunting, and moored it slap opposite the palace at Whitehall. Amused rather than annoyed at this piece of presumption, Charles granted him a pension along with a commission in the navy; his ship, renamed *The Royal Escape*, was taken into the fleet as an unarmed 'smack'. Tettersell was later given command of a frigate and carried out various escort duties. But he was eventually dismissed the service for 'unbecoming behaviour' during a naval engagement.

This misdemeanour did not prevent Tettersell from being elected Constable of Brighthelmstone, an office he apparently performed 'with the zeal of the bigot and the malign industry of a ministerial spy', making himself as unpleasant as he could to everyone around him. In particular, he seems to have made a point of persecuting dissenters. On one occasion, it is related, being infuriated by the lightness of the £50 fine imposed by the Lewes magistrates on some Quakers who had been convicted—on the basis of his own false evidence—of holding a meeting, he broke into the malthouse belonging to one of the Quakers, held a sale of the contents, and pocketed the proceeds. Likewise he seems to have nourished a grudge against Gaius Smith, at whose tavern Charles had put up on the night of his escape.

Possibly this may have been through a reluctance to share the credit of having helped the King, though Smith never claimed any reward for his loyalty. Or it may simply have been a case of professional jealousy. For in his affluent days after the Restoration, Tettersell became the landlord of another 'George' inn located in Middle Street—the opposition, as it were. And then in 1670 he acquired a more substantial property 'containing by estimation one road the Old Shipp & in the Hempshires'. This was the Old Ship Hotel, and since it represents the intellectual focus of our story let us pause for a moment to get the gist of its background.

'The earliest record of [the Old Ship], dated 1559, is the first for any inn in Brighton, and its beginnings may go back to early Tudor times,' affirms the local historian, Clifford Musgrave. 'The origin of its name is uncertain, but it most probably derives from the inn having been constructed, at least in part, from the timbers of an old vessel. A piece of carved timber which appears to have been part of a ship's stern for many years formed part of the entrance to the stables . . . perhaps one wrecked upon the shore at Brighton.'

In her monograph on the hotel, Judy Middleton adds: 'People who are familiar with the Old Ship's position on the seafront today may be surprised to learn that in its early days it was not by the sea at all, but tucked away in a side street in the centre of Brighthelmstone. It is not that the Old Ship has moved from the original site in Ship Street (although of course it has expanded from it over the years) but that the sea and a series of storms swept away the old houses built under the cliff to the south of the King's Road. The hotel traces its ancestry back to a tavern known simply as the Ship. It is possible that this tavern first opened its doors in the days of Queen Elizabeth I because there is a record of a cottage in the Hempshires being owned by a Richard and a John Gilham in 1559 and we know that two later Gilhams were owners of the Ship.'

In those days this was the area where hemp was grown to supply the rope-makers of Brighton, and Ship Street was known as Ye Hempshires until it took its name from the town's most prominent inn in the eighteenth century. Long before that, however, the Ship had been obliged to alter its own name when another tavern was built almost opposite and unimaginatively—it seems to have been a habit in these parts—chose the same appellation. From 1650, therefore, the original tavern was known as the Old Ship, and the upstart youngster the New Ship.

One wonders what the locals made of Nicholas Tettersell in his role of proprietor, for by all accounts he was hardly the type to make a genial Mine Host. However, as it turned out, his tenure was brief. When he died four years later, he made sure that the tavern remained in the family by leaving it to his daughter Susanna, who was married to a certain John Geering; and his grand-daughter Susanna, the wife of Dr Peter White of Lewes, inherited the property in 1714.

In the mystique of most localities some particular adventure has been absorbed, and become familiar to every schoolchild. So it is appropriate that pictures of Charles II should hang on Brighton schoolroom walls. Not only did he put this little fishing village on the map, but as a character he was very much in tune with the lively town to which he unwittingly became sponsor. Yet it must be admitted that Charles (to say nothing of the ennobled ladies who sought his more intimate favours) did more to promote places like Tunbridge Wells, whither his frolicking court removed to escape from plague-infested London, and even Epsom—where he installed Nell Gwyn in a nearby tavern to avoid time hanging too heavily on his hands—than he ever did for Brighton. Clearly the town's rise to fame must be ascribed less to him than to the subsequent prince who made it his home and stamped the imprint of his Regency on a whole era.

And what of Nick Tettersell? By all accounts he seems to have been a bully and a boor. For all this, he was the first local man to emerge as a distinctive figure; and even if he was not really, as he liked to believe, the hero of the day on that Wednesday, 15 October 1651, at least he provided the means by which the King escaped. Had he not played his part, through both loyalty and greed, the history of England might well have been different. So as we meet in the Old Ship Bar that bears his name, let us give his portrait a nod as we hoist a convivial brew.

CHAPTER 3

The Ocean's Healing Waters

In the Brighton Museum can be seen the dark grey neolithic pots of the earliest known dwellers in this area—the so-called Windmill Hill culture, whose settlements were on the high ground behind the town—along with an elegant Bronze Age cup, carved from a single piece of translucent amber, which was dug up in what is now Palmeira Avenue in Hove. And on the road to Ditchling you can climb over one of the Iron Age hill-forts, built in the third century BC; while at the corner of Preston and Springfield roads lie the remains of a Roman farmhouse. Yet of Brighton's early history there is not a great deal to be said. Though the Anglo-Saxons seem to have been the first to create a settlement of any size here after the landing of Aella and his sons near Selsey in AD 477, the first overlord of which any record exists was Wulnoth, who repelled a Danish invasion in 1008 and whose son Godwin was created Earl of Kent, Surrey and Sussex. In the Domesday Book 'Bristelmestune' formed part of the Barony of Lewes; its 90 inhabitants paid an annual rental of 4,000 herrings. Later, in the fourteenth century, it was the venue for a market, and a fair on the feast of St Bartholomew. But throughout all these centuries, even at the time of Charles II's escapade, Brighton remained an isolated little world whose bones were shingle, whose blood was the sea, whose hair the treeless turf of the Downs, and (to pursue the metaphor) whose thoughts ran to little more than herrings, whose eyes were always focused on the horizon, fearful of raiders . . .

Never was it free of attacks from the sea. In retaliation for the despoiling of their own land, the French landed near Brighton at Rottingdean in 1377

2. Dr Richard Russell put Brighton on the map as a health resort and it was in 1750 that he published his book on the use of sea-water in treating certain diseases. Looking at this portrayal when he was old and toothless, it is hard to visualise the dashing young man who had eloped with an heiress. William Hicks of the Old Ship commissioned Benjamin Wilson to paint the portrait (doubtless out of gratitude for the increase in business). It hung for many years in the Ballroom, until it was presented in 1887 to Brighton Corporation by the then proprietors, Robert Bacon and his brother-in-law, Samuel Ridley

and ravaged the whole countryside from Portsmouth to Hastings, carrying off the Prior of Lewes as a prisoner; a century and a half later, when Henry VIII was quarrelling with Louis XII, raids were commonplace and one night in June 1514 the French burnt the whole town, leaving only the church standing. A drawing of this unhappy event, though more entertaining than accurate, shows a stoutly-walled quadrangle of pebblestone cottages with sloping tiled roofs built in parallel rows that ran over the white cliffs and extended right down to the water.

Marauders apart, the sea itself was a hostile element. The lower part of the town was built on a spit of land from which the sea had retreated centuries before; but over the centuries it reversed its action, gradually eroding the low cliff-line to such an extent that at least half the medieval town, including the blockhouse and its quaintly-named 'gun-garden', was swept away by the water. After the great storms of 1703 and 1705 Daniel Defoe was inspired to write a treatise on 'The exhalation, dilation and extension of winds', observing that 'Brighthelmstone being an old built and poor, tho' populous town, was miserably torn to pieces, and made the very picture of desolation, that it looked as if an enemy had sacked it'.

Traditionally there was friction between the fisherfolk of the lower town and the farming community. The fishermen—helped by some smuggling on the side—formed the more prosperous majority, whereas the landsmen, as they were called, had a hard time keeping sheep and growing corn on the Downs. They were hampered by droughts, for there were no streams in the area apart from the Wellsbourne, which dried up in the summer.

Since the corn was poor, and the animals few, Brighthelmstone existed on fish. Consequently the fishermen governed the town which, comments Sir Osbert Sitwell, was 'ruled internally by a despotic body, only comparable to the dreaded Council of Ten in Venice'.

Here it was known as 'The Society of Twelve', nominally the 'ancientest gravest and wisest' who were chosen once a year by the three churchwardens, and its job was to elect a Constable. In practice this dignitary was drawn exclusively from the ranks of the fishermen, who re-elected one another without any regard to the wishes of the rest of the population. Of the Constable's arbitrary power, Captain Tettersell bore witness.

In the early days of the eighteenth century Brighton was in a wretched state, still an insignificant little fishing village of no more than a thousand inhabitants and virtually ignored by the rest of the county. For, as Colonel Gounter had said, even those who lived only a mile or two inland took no notice of the sea. Like the Scottish highlands and indeed the Alps, it was considered beyond the pale by civilised men.

Yet this attitude was to change. As the century progressed, the taste for spas was extended to the hitherto neglected 'seaside'. Doctors began to recommend the virtues of sea-water treatment, and the eminent physician Sir John Floyer (1649–1734) published a couple of learned books entitled *An Inquiry into the use of Baths* and a *History of Cold Bathing*. At Scarborough, whose mineral spring was on the foreshore, venturesome spirits plunged naked into the water from small boats, and mixed bathing parties were held on the beach; while Beale's 'bathing machines', dragged by horses, conveyed men and women into the brine at Margate.

From the Rev. William Clarke, we have a glimpse of Brighton at the time: 'We are now sunning ourselves upon the beach at Brighthelmstone,' wrote the Rector of Buxted in a letter dated July 1736. 'Such a tract of sea; such regions of corn; and such an extent of fine carpet, that gives your eye the command of it all. But then the mischief is, that we have little communication besides the *clamor nauticus*, which is here a sort of treble to the plashing of the waves against the cliffs.

'My morning business is bathing in the sea, and then buying fish; the evening is riding out for air, viewing the remains of old Saxon camps and counting the ships in the road and the boats that are trawling. Sometimes we give the imagination leave to expatiate a little—fancy that you are coming down, and that we intend to dine one day in Dieppe.'

A weekly cross-channel service had been inaugurated from Brighton to Dieppe by sailing packet, but the rector regarded such a trip as an alarming adventure. Meanwhile, he told his correspondent, they were living almost underground. 'I fancy the architects here usually take the altitude of the inhabitants and lose not an inch between the head and the ceiling, and then dropping a step or two below the surface, the second storey is finished in something under 12 feet.' This, he supposed, was a necessary precaution against storms, so that the inhabitants would not be blown out of bed into New England, Barbary or God knows where else. 'But as the lodgings are low,' he conceded, 'they are cheap; we have two parlours, two bed-chambers, pantry, etc. for five shillings a week; and if you will really come down you need not fear a bed of the proper dimensions. And then the coast is safe; the cannons are all covered with rust and grass; the ships are moored, and no enemy apprehended.'

Another visitor was Dr John Burton, an Oxford lecturer, who had difficulty travelling over the notoriously bad Sussex roads—nothing more than cattle drivers' tracks, he thought, so ubiquitous were the footmarks of oxen. 'Why is it that the oxen, the swine, the women, and all other animals are so long-legged in Sussex?' he quipped in his donnish way. 'Might the difficulty of pulling the feet out of so much mud have lengthened their bones?'

Brighton itself seemed quite lively as he engaged a room at the Old Ship Inn, and ordered his supper. But the people appeared to be needy and wretched—most of them looked like seamen—and their houses were squat. From the inn you got an uninterrupted view of the sea, for the buildings that once stood in front of it had been swept away into a huge heap of fallen masonry. Wooden groins had been erected to protect the houses that remained, and though Daniel Defoe had considered that they were not worth saving, Dr Burton thought them adequate enough. But he found the place too noisy for comfort. After eating like 'the heroes of Homer after a battle' he was kept awake most of the night by drunken sailors 'singing out with their barbarous voices, clapping and making all manner of noises', to say nothing of the women 'quarrelling and fighting about their fish'.

Such was the scene when, just a hundred years after Charles II made his escape from the town, Dr Russell began sending patients to Brighton for his sea-water cure—the novelty of which consisted not just in wallowing about in the sea, but of drinking the sea-water too.

A native of Lewes, Russell had eloped with the only daughter of William Kemp, whose family we shall be encountering again later; and after studying medicine at Leyden University under the celebrated Dutch physician Herman Boerhaave, he returned to practise as a doctor at Lewes. There, like his mentor, he achieved distinction by the publication in 1749 of a learned treatise entitled *De Tabe Glandulari; sui De Usu Aquae Marinae in Morbis Glandularum Dissertatio*, a title less daunting when translated into vernacular English as *Dissertation on the Use of Sea-Water in diseases of the Glands*. Both were published under the imprimatur of the Vice-Chancellor of Oxford University, which gave them academic respectability (and perhaps entitles Oxford to be considered a sponsor of Brighton!).

Invoking the names of Pliny, Hippocrates, Celsus and other learned sources, Dr Russell claimed to have 'brought a medicine of the ancient Physicians again into practice', and so wide-ranging were his experiments with concoctions of crabs' eyes, coral, burnt sponge, cuttlefish bones, viper's flesh and woodlice, so recondite were the prescriptions to be washed down with a pint of sea-water, so startling were the cures attributed to them, that a flood of visitors began making its way to Brighton. His cure probably owed more to the bracing sea air and the detergent effect of the sea-water on eighteenth-century grime than to the healing properties of woodlice and crabs' eyes; but people with overfed constitutions had yet to learn that a good purge and a dose of ozone were all they really needed—Dr Brighton, in fact, as Thackeray was later to proclaim.

The success of his treatment prompted Russell to build an impressive red brick and white stone house on the site now occupied by the Royal Albion Hotel. With its arched windows and pedimented doorway opening out on to the Steine, Russell House was a cut above everything else in the town; later, when rented by the Duke of Cumberland, it was to become the centre of fashionable society. And once comfortably installed as resident physician, conveniently near the beach for patients who lodged with him, Dr Russell widened the range of his activities. Before long an egregiously named 'oceanic fluid' was being bottled and sold at Tunbridge Wells and other inland towns; advertisements in the London press announced that 'Sea Water took off the ocean from Brighthelmstone' could be procured at the Talbot Inn in Southwark. But not everyone was prepared to drink Brighton's precious sea-water, which must have been a particularly unpleasant emetic; many invalids preferred waters from mineral springs. Fortuitously, therefore, Dr Russell was able to discover a chalybeate spring known as St Ann's Well just west of the town at Hove; and once enclosed inside a Grecian-style Pumproom, this pleasant little spa—whose waters seem to have had roughly the same properties as those of Tunbridge Wells—greatly enhanced Brighton's status as a health resort. People who were bored with the Pantiles at Tunbridge Wells could continue their cure there and have a dip in the sea as well.

If a hint of commercialism lingers around Dr Russell's activities, he was far from being a quack. On the contrary, his sea-cure made a great impression in medical circles. He was elected a Fellow of the Royal Society, and in a poem published soon after his death, Michelet called him 'l'inventeur de la Mer'.

Certainly he laid the groundwork for Brighton's future prosperity, and remains firmly enshrined as the city's first great benefactor, even if his son took a more light-hearted view:

Brighthelmstone was confessed by all
T'abound with females fair,
But more so since fam'd Russell has
Preferred the waters there.

Then fly that dangerous town ye swains
For fear ye shall endure
A pain from some bright sparkling eye
Which Russell's skill can't cure.

3. The chalybeate spring at Hove was recommended to patients by two eminent doctors, Dr Richard Russell and Dr Anthony Relham. The latter stated that 'bodies labouring under the consequences of irregular living and illicit pleasure' would be much relieved by drinking the water. If patients found it really unpalatable they could drink it warmed. Mrs Fitzherbert was one of the fashionable crowd who frequented the spring

But if Dr Russell invented the Brighton sea, his successor discovered the Brighton climate. Dr Anthony Relham, the Irishman who took over most of his practice, began by publishing a guide to the place, with *Remarks on its Air and Analysis of its Waters*, which extolled the virtues of the soil and weather. Observing how fresh breezes blew in summer and warm sea winds banished frost, he went on to add that the town was luckily 'distant from the noxious streams of perspiring trees'; and moreover that the absence of any river made the chalky soil dry and the air very pure. What's more, the lack of rivers meant that the sea was saltier than at any other seaside place.

Warming to the blarney, he recommended that waters at St Ann's Well should be drunk with caution, being liable to stimulate 'an increase of appetite and spirits'; he had observed that 'bodies labouring under the consequences of irregular living and illicit pleasures were greatly relieved' by the waters. He mentioned, too, the unusual fecundity of the sheep which drank them, but refrained from comment as to the effect on human beings.

It was left to his colleague, Dr John Awsiter, to promote the value of sea-water in cases of barrenness. 'There is a fecundity in sea-water beyond even the much famed mud of the River Nile' was the opinion expressed in a pamphlet published by the third of these medical men of letters.

Realising, however, that the bracing wind and pebbly beach might be a shade too rigorous for invalids and timid ladies, Dr Awsiter proceeded to erect a building containing hot sea-water baths. Heat, he pointed out, enabled the pores of the skin to open and allowed the 'poisonous humours' to be released; and he further tempered the rigours of the cure by permitting his patients to dilute their daily dose of salt water with milk. (Ugh!)

These promotional efforts had gratifying results, not least because an increasing number of visitors who went for treatment of the body found that the seaside was a medicine for the soul. Though the sea-water cure may not have been quite the panacea that it was claimed to be, there was no doubt that the sick tended to perk up and the robust became heartier. If nothing else, it gave point to Floyer's dictum: 'Cold bathing has this good alone. It makes old John to hug old Joan.' And as time went on, we hear less about treatments and salt-water draughts, but plenty about the pleasures of the Brighton scene.

CHAPTER 4

Agrémens by the Sea

This town, or village of renown
Like London Bridge, half broken down,
Few years ago was worse than Wapping
Not fit for human soul to stop in;
But now, like a worn-out shoe,
By patching well, the place will do.
You'd wonder much, I'm sure, to see
How it's becrammed with quality;
Here Lords and Ladies oft carouse,
Together in a tiny house . . .
And what his valet would despise,
His lordship praises to the skies,
But such the ton is, such the case,
You'll see the first of rank or place,
With star and riband, all profuse,
Duck at his door-way like a goose.

George Saville Carey, 1777

4. This rare print of 1828 shows the Ballroom of the Old Ship where the Prince Regent once danced. It was built in the 1750s and was the largest room in Brighton being 90 feet in length. Not surprisingly it proved to be so popular that it became necessary to build on a Card Room which was completed in 1767. The most remarkable feature of the Ballroom was the balcony which held the musicians and hung apparently without any support against the wall. In 1801 the windows were draped in pink calico with tasselled pelmets and the chairs had green moreen cushions

When passing through Brighton on his tour, Defoe had few kindly words for the crumbling cliffs, the ruined fortifications, the tumbledown cottages and the general appearance of decay. Yet this was just what enchanted the fashionable world when it discovered the little place a few decades later. The narrow unpaved streets, the cramped dark lodgings in which they bumped their heads against the low beams, the fishing nets they had to scramble over, all held the same attraction for these elegant folk, observes Osbert Sitwell, as the modish longing for rustic solitude and simplicity that was taking shape across the water in the Petit Trianon where the blasé inhabitants of Versailles, under the garb of Maître Jacques le Meunier or Fanchette la Laitière, milked cows and herded sheep with silver-gilt crooks (to say nothing of gambolling among the haystacks). But fortunately no revolution was brewing under their feet in Brighton, as it was for Marie Antoinette and the Comte d'Artois. On the contrary, the local tradesmen and fisherfolk were only too happy to pocket the easy money that came their way for looking after the visitors' needs.

Looking back, it must have been very much the same story two hundred years ago at Brighton as we ourselves have witnessed at Marbella, Moustique, Tuscany and other idyllic spots that have caught the discriminating eye. Before long the fishing village was being spruced up and the masons were busy. 'It improves daily,' we find Dr Relham writing in 1761, 'as the inhabitants, encouraged by the late resort of company, seem disposed to expend the whole of what they acquire in making new buildings, or making the old ones convenient.'

Nowhere can the town's emancipation into a fashionable resort be followed better than at the Old Ship Inn, which was still the leading, and indeed the only, acceptable tavern. Between 1714 and 1733 it changed hands five times, which hardly said much for its value as a going concern. Though the contents were valued at £200 in 1717, William Hicks, who ran a brewery in Black Lion Street, was able to acquire the whole property in 1733 for a mere £84.

As things turned out, he bought at the right time. For the next 20 years the Old Ship had the field to itself, and Hicks must have done very well, offering everything from cock-fights to dances. Already we hear of a ball that was held at the Old Ship in January 1751, at which 21 couples were present. Proceedings were opened by the High Sheriff of Sussex, Robert Ball of Chichester, who led off a contre-danse with an heiress from Lewes, aptly named Miss Treadwell, to the tune of 'The Sow in the Sack' (also not inappropriate, for he subsequently married her).

But in 1755 a rival appeared in the shape of the Castle. Originally opened up in a private house on the Steine, the Castle Tavern was rebuilt and greatly enlarged ten years later, swallowing up the Fountain Inn next door. And in a bid to capture the patronage of the wealthy and fashionable crowd that was now coming to Brighton, its enterprising owner, Samuel Shergold, commissioned John Crunden to design a magnificent ballroom.

Such an Assembly Room, nearly always on the first floor with a window leading on to the top of the porch, was of course a Georgian convention, the venue for functions, dinners and dances. The Old Ship already possessed one, for it is mentioned in William Hicks' will dated 20 November 1759. But when John Hicks inherited the property from his father in 1765 and found himself faced with stiff competition from Shergold, he decided to improve the hotel's amenities. It seems likely, suggests Judy Middleton, that there were actually three phases of development: first the ballroom, then the 'handsome Coffee-Room . . . and capacious Dining Room' and finally the Card Room, designed by Robert Golden.

The Old Ship's Ballroom with its flat coved ceiling was the largest room

1. Portrait of Charles II

2. Portrait of Nicholas Tettersell

3. The *Royal Escape* after van de Velde

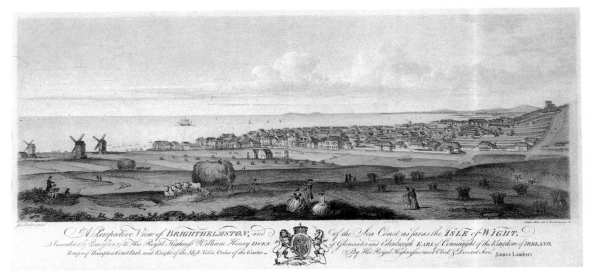

4. Lambert's View of Brighthelmston in 1765

5. Portrait of the Prince of Wales by
van der Puyl

in Brighton. Ninety feet long, its most remarkable features were a balcony for spectators at one end, and a carved musicians' gallery with delicate ironwork railings in the centre. Writing in 1824 Sicklemore could not get over the sight of an orchestra playing on a balcony that 'hung apparently without any support against the wall', and the same disregard for gravity strikes us even today. Around the walls were benches covered with green moreen cushions; four lofty pier-glasses reflected the light from three chandeliers. The Dining Room next door was decorated with murals depicting the story of Telemachus painted in bronze tones on a blue background, and the shallow vaulted ceiling of the Card Room, with its plasterwork garlands, reeded mouldings and Adamesque panels, echoed this classical theme.

For sheer splendour the Old Ship's Assembly Rooms, asserts Relham, were 'not to be excelled, perhaps, by any in England, that of York excepted'. They were 'more neat and commodious, though possibly less elegant' than those built for the Castle Inn by Crunden, who later designed that most charming of buildings, Boodle's Club in St James's. The walls of the Castle Ballroom, we are told, were decorated with plaster reliefs like Wedgwood cameos, with delicate mouldings and scrolls; the shallow arched ceiling was similar to that in the Subscription Room in Brooks's Club.

Here then was elegance on a metropolitan scale to tempt the exquisites from London! From 1767 onwards the public assemblies, balls and promenades that became such an agreeable feature of Brighton life took place in these rooms, whereas daytime activities revolved around the bookshops.

5. The Castle Inn was the great rival to the Old Ship. Each had a large room for Balls and Assemblies and the establishments sensibly arranged for their functions to be held on different evenings so they did not clash. The Castle Ballroom came to an unusual end when it was converted to a chapel royal in 1821. The Prince Regent had left the previous chapel royal in North Street after a tactless sermon by the vicar on the subject of Bathsheba

33

Foreigners were often surprised by the British fondness for books. 'The national authors are in all hands, and read by all people,' observed young Pastor Moritz, who toured England in 1782, 'My landlady, who is only a taylor's widow, reads her Milton; and tells me that her late husband fell in love with her on this very account.' But though the purveying of fiction was their ostensible purpose, it was the least of the libraries' functions. They were, especially in resorts, the hub of society—public clubs where men and women could meet and gossip at a time when taverns and drawing-rooms would otherwise have kept them segregated for much of the day. Like the print shops in London—such as Fores in Piccadilly, Holland's in Drury Lane and Ackermann's in the Strand—they became an indispensable part of everyday life, being equipped with comfortable lounges in which folios could be studied, and exhibitions were held.

The first to be seen in Brighton appeared in 1760 when a Mr Baker came down from Tunbridge Wells and built a pleasant white-painted wooden bookshop on the eastern side of the Steine. On its arched verandah ladies in modishly high headdresses foregathered to exchange tit-bits of scandal, smiling meaningfully behind their fans as their eyes slyly followed the tail-coated gentlemen who strolled up and down the lawns.

To add to the amenities, Mr Baker also erected a small bandstand, somewhat grandly called the Rotunda, under which a trombone and two French horns disseminated sweet but penetrating refrains. On fine after-noons, indeed, they could be heard on the other side of the Steine, where in due course another bookshop opened up, along with a number of small tourist shops selling toys, knick-knacks, lace and millinery—a foretaste of Brighton's ubiquitous 'kitsch korners'. Often they disposed of their stock by means of raffles, astutely implying that expensive smuggled goods could be acquired by simply staking a small sum against the fall of a dice. With lace in such demand for both male and female attire, the chance of lighting on a bargain held an irresistible appeal.

If the rattle of the dice was to be heard all day long on the Steine, gambling in the libraries concentrated on 'Loo', a form of sweepstake played with cards. True, energetic characters rode on the firm turf of the Downs, sometimes coursing with the local pack of harriers or hunting deer that had been released for that purpose. There were also the Lewes races, and private competitions that were held a mile or two from Brighton on Whitehawk Down. We hear of Hicks' horse being matched for ten guineas against that of Dr Kipping (a man obviously not to be trifled with, for he once fought an impromptu duel in the middle of West Street with an army officer, and confiscated his sword).

Regular cock-fights, too, were staged at both the Old Ship and the Castle Tavern, along with bull-baiting at Rottingdean. But the more indolent souls spent their days around the libraries, glancing through portfolios, tinkling on the harpsichord, gambling for shilling stakes, making up card parties, or playing billiards—the ladies in particular seem to have handled their cues with a grace and accuracy that would have astonished later generations.

Here, too, were kept the visitors' books in which newcomers were required to write their names and pay a fee before they could receive invitations for the Assemblies, which were organised and presided over by a

Master of Ceremonies. This appointment was an indication of the expanding social scene; to prevent clashes John Hicks and Samuel Shergold agreed to call in Captain Wade from Bath, where the season conveniently ended just as Brighton's summer activities began. Wade's duty was to arrange the principal balls and assemblies, which were held alternately at the Old Ship and the Castle Inn.

In practice Wade quickly elevated himself to the position of being the arbiter of social affairs, following Beau Nash's 'Rules of Conduct' almost to the letter; and though their tone was more of persuasion than command they were disregarded at one's peril. Indeed so pompous was his manner, so authoritarian his edicts on matters of dress and behaviour, that Wade soon became almost as celebrated at Brighton as Nash had been in Bath some years earlier. 'Mothers with marriageable daughters were anxious to stand in his good graces; the unprotected maiden of uncertain age, the lone dowager, reluctant to relinquish her waning opportunities of shining in society, each sheltered under his aegis; portionless sons, or it may be needy adventurers, assiduously sought his favour,' observed the historian Bishop. In due course Wade left Bath under a cloud, and though he became equally unpopular at Brighton, the task of shepherding a growing flock of frivolous visitors through an increasing number of social events can hardly have been easy. Apart from the weekly balls—on Mondays at the Castle and every Thursday at the Old Ship—there were card assemblies four times a week at which from 200 to 300 people took part, and on Sundays a Promenade and Public Tea at the Assembly Rooms. This was a sort of fashion parade until a bell rang and the company split up into parties for tea.

Though already so fashionable, the town was still only half a square mile of buildings with six principal streets, bounded by Mr Baker's bookshop—later to become Thomas's Library—on the far side of the Steine and a view of downland on the other. Tall new buildings, somewhat out of scale with the scruffy little cottages beside them, gave the streets a hugger-mugger look likened by a commentator to 'the gums of a child in the process of losing his milk-teeth and acquiring secondary ones'. These new houses were all built with their backs to the sea, which was still considered a desolate prospect compared to the elegant spectacle of the Steine. They were built of flint and brick; the few that have survived consist of a single main room on each floor enlivened by window bays that ran through two or three storeys—a reminder that the charming bow windows introduced by Robert Adam first became popular in Brighton.

Most of them were built as lodgings from the start. Yet so great was the demand for accommodation that many people had to make do with appallingly cramped quarters. Though he found the sea-bathing delightful and proposed to stay for as long as the weather held good, 'Gilly' Williams warned his friend George Selwyn that even the best lodgings were execrable, and 'what you would find now, I believe, not habitable'. Since nearly 500 subscribers crammed themselves into a Ball at the Old Ship in 1768, the crush can be imagined.

By now the town was becoming studded with the great names which henceforth were to mark every stage of its development. In 1771 the Duke of Marlborough acquired a newly built house standing between Dr Russell's abode and the old Manor house at the south end of the Steine, where he

George the fourth, then Prince of Wales, first went to Brighton in 1782, on a visit to the Duke of Cumberland. The original Pavilion was commenced in 1784, and finished in 1787. It was built on the site of the house known as "Mr Scrase's".

The Steyne at Brighton in 1778.

6. *The Steine as it was in 1778. Even before the Prince Regent made Brighton famous, the place was well patronised by society. The Duke of Marlborough had bought a house in 1771, the Duke and Duchess of Argyle visited Brighton in 1778 and when the Duke and Duchess of Cumberland arrived the following year, the bells were rung in welcome. On the east side of the Steine stood Thomas's Library which was popular enough to stay open all the year. The annual subscription for borrowing books was 10s 6d*

established himself with a retinue of 40 servants. Though the richest peer in England, he had no hesitation in letting off the rooms separately when he was away, so that as many as 50 people were put up at the same time.

The Duke and Duchess were quiet folk, their habits being in marked contrast with the leaders of the *ton*. They hardly ventured out except to stroll on the Steine. But the Manor house next door belonged to a gouty old solicitor named Richard Scrase, an intimate friend of the Thrales. Mrs Thrale is chiefly remembered, of course, for her anecdotes of Dr Samuel Johnson, who was virtually a member of the Thrale household at Streatham for 16 years, and it was she and her husband who first brought the Doctor to Brighton in 1765.

He was then 55. Sadly his sensations on catching his first sight of the sea have not been recorded, but apparently he swam with enough enthusiasm to warrant a backhanded compliment from his dipper. 'Why, Sir,' exclaimed the redoubtable 'Smoaker' Miles, 'You must have been a stout-hearted gentleman forty years ago!' Dr Johnson also rode Mrs Thrale's old hunter, following the harriers with such determination that one of the huntsmen remarked admiringly, 'Johnson rides as well as the most illiterate young sportsman in England'.

'I am better pleased with that compliment,' chuckled the Doctor, 'than any I have ever received.' He would cover 50 miles without getting tired, Mrs Thrale tells us, but would never admit to enjoying it. 'Hunting is not a diversion at all,' he observed testily, 'It is very strange and melancholy that the paucity of human pleasures should persuade us ever to call hunting of them.' Indeed few of Brighton's fashionable amusements appealed to him.

'You hunt in the morning,' he grumbled, 'and crowd the rooms at night, and call it diversion, when your heart knows it is perishing for poverty of pleasures and your wits get blunted for want of some other mind to sharpen them upon.'

The truth is that Samuel Johnson was never really happy out of London. If he came to Brighton, it was perhaps in the hope that Dr Russell's sea-water cure might heal his skin infection, but chiefly to be with his friends the Thrales. Yet he soon became bored: for so inveterate a Londoner the place was still too small to offer the intellectual entertainment he craved. As a result he was more than usually grumpy, mercilessly mauling people like Russell's grandson, Dr Pepys. 'The moment the cloth was removed,' relates Pepys of one verbal encounter, 'he challenged me to come out, as he called it, and say what I had to object to in his Life of Lord Lyttelton. I could not but obey, and so to it we went for three or four hours without ceasing.' It was a frightful scene, says Fanny Burney, 'I never saw Dr Johnson really in a passion but then. He so red, poor Mr Pepys so pale.'

Another victim was the local rector. Dr Michell had an unfortunate tendency to discourse about his internal ailments, but he did not expect to be cut short with the words: 'Dear Doctor, do not be like a spider and spin conversation thus incessantly out of thy own bowels.'

When the dust had settled, the rector retaliated on the subject of personal hygiene. According to Mrs Thrale, Johnson could never be persuaded to change his shirt before it became indispensably necessary. 'I saw Michell of Brighthelmstone affront Johnson about fleas,' she relates. 'Why Sir,' came the answer, 'Why should not flea bite o' me be treated as phlebotomy? It empties the capillary vessels.'

As a devout churchman, Johnson put up with the rector's sermons, but away from the pulpit he believed in a 'good solid knock-down argument'. One evening at the Old Ship Assembly rooms, while the rest of the company were enjoying a country dance, the two of them stood by the fireplace chatting amicably enough until, provoked by some clerical remark, Johnson raised his voice—at the best of times powerful. Not to be outdone by mere decibels, the rector took up a poker and banged the grate to emphasise his point; whereupon Johnson seized the tongs and did likewise. Between them they made such a din that the dancers stopped in alarm, to be greeted by the sight of their man of God and the 'Grand Cham' of literature hammering away like a couple of demented children, until Captain Wade intervened and quietened the two old gentlemen down.

No doubt there were other incidents that Mrs Thrale omitted to mention, and it is a pity that Boswell never saw the inside of her house in West Street. But he did receive a letter from Brighthelmstone dated 9 Sept 1769 which contained a pertinent observation: 'There is between the history and the journal that difference which there will always be found between notions borrowed without, and notions generated within. Your history was copied from books: your journal rose out of your own experience and observation.' On this occasion Johnson was in no hurry to leave Brighthelmstone. 'I do not find that I am likely to come back very soon from this place. I shall, perhaps, stay a fortnight longer.' But by December 1782 the old man was feeling his 73 years. 'Having passed almost this whole year in a succession of disorders,' he told Boswell, 'I went in October to Brighthelm-

7. The eminent Dr Samuel Johnson in a suitably crusty mood. While staying at Brighton he practically came to blows with the rector and grumbled at the lack of trees, stating that if one became depressed at having to live in such a desolate spot 'it would be difficult to find a tree on which to fasten the rope'. In short Brighton did not charm him—the reason he came was because his good friends the Thrales had a house in West Street

8. A delightful portrait of Hester Thrale as a young woman. In addition to her looks she had an intellect powerful enough to keep Dr Johnson as a devoted friend for many years. The friendship ended because the aged doctor felt slighted when the recently widowed Hester began to take a great interest in the Italian musician Piozzi, whom she subsequently married

stone whither I came in a state of so much weakness, that I rested four times in walking between the inn and the lodging. By physick and abstinence I grew better, and am now reasonably easy, though at a great distance from health.' Yet his mood was so depressed that he found Brighton unspeakably dull—'So truly desolate that if one had a mind to hang oneself for desperation on being obliged to live there, it would be difficult to find a tree on which to fasten the rope,' he remarked caustically to his hostess.

In contrast Edward Gibbon (the two men never could see eye to eye) enjoyed Brighton and found the society 'good and easy'. To recuperate after publishing the third volume of his *History*, Gibbon had taken a little house overlooking the sea for the summer. 'The air gives health, spirits and a ravenous appetite,' he wrote to his stepmother. 'I walk sufficiently morning and evening, lounge in the middle of the day on the Steine, booksellers' shops, etc., and by the help of a pair of horses can make distant excursions.' Also 'after due preparation and advice' he bathed in the sea. But when he returned later that year with Lord and Lady Sheffield he was bound to admit that there was a difference between the sunshine of August and the cold fogs of November. 'Instead of my beautiful seashore, I am confined to a dark lodging in the middle of the town, for the place is still full,' he sighed. To make matters worse, Lord Sheffield was called away, leaving poor Gibbon 'in the servile state of a married man' and obliged to spend his time escorting Lady Sheffield around 'in the dull imitation of a London life'.

Revelling, however, in the social round that this unwilling cicisbeo found such heavy going was another literary figure: for the demure-looking young lady staying with the Thrales was the authoress of a best-selling novel. So shy and retiring was Fanny Burney before she married and became Madame d'Arblay, that she might have passed unnoticed had it not been for Mrs Thrale, who never let the company forget that her guest had written *Evelina*, the most celebrated book of the day.

From our point of view this is of less immediate interest than Miss Burney's *Diary*, which introduces us to some of the figures who were to be seen on the Steine and in the Assembly Rooms. Lord Mordault, Fanny thought, was a 'pretty, languid, townish young man'; Sir Philip Clarke a 'wit and libertine'; Gerald Hamilton—the MP whose one devastating utterance in Parliament earned him the sobriquet 'Single-speech Hamilton'—struck her as intelligent, dry, sarcastic and clever. The 'gaily sociable' Bishop of Peterborough contrasted with the smug and reserved Rector of Lewes; Lady Pembroke and Lady Diana Beauclerk both had 'still very pleasing remains of beauty' (though they might not have been happy to hear it expressed in quite that way); Mrs Masters was the reigning toast of the season; but everyone laughed at the 'tonnish graces and impertinencies' of the playwright Richard Cumberland's family, sporting powdered and pomaded coiffures topped by feathers that reached 3 feet above their foreheads. (Later, when Cumberland was appointed envoy to Madrid, the arrival of his daughters at the Escorial caused such a stir among the Spanish guards that he had to send them home.)

Because, too, of periodic invasion scares a regiment of the Sussex Militia had been quartered in the town, whose officers could usually be seen strolling among the ladies on the Steine. (The ranks, no doubt, made off with their girls to some more secluded spot.)

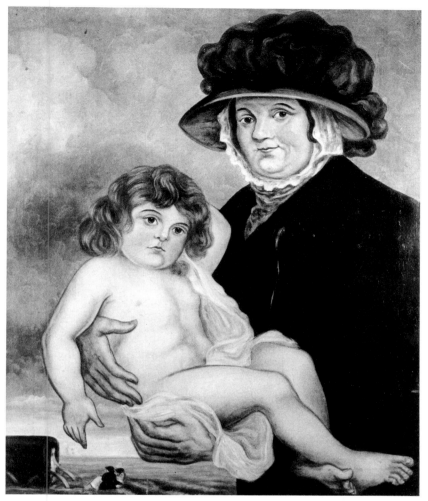

9. *Martha Gunn was Brighton's most famous dipper—that is, a woman who attended ladies bathing in the sea. In later years she grew to be as round as a dumpling but being well covered must have been an advantage and helped her to withstand the chill of being continually in and out of the sea. In this painting by J. Broughton she is shown holding the infant George IV which is interesting, because he did not come to Brighton until 1783 when he was 21 years old and when he did bathe, his attendant was a man called Smoaker Miles*

The officers' mess was in the Old Ship Tavern, and hardly had Miss Burney unpacked her bags than an invitation to dine with them came her way, along with the Thrales. After an excellent meal they were taken out to the parade ground where their host's company was being mustered. It was all delightfully informal, for the men were so drunk they could hardly stand upright, added to which the wind blew the ladies' dresses around in a way that had the soldiers convulsed with uncontrollable giggles. 'The poor fellows have just been paid their arrears, and it is so unusual for them to have a sixpence in their pockets that they know not how to keep it there,' explained the young officer, who after an unsuccessful attempt to restore order burst out laughing himself. Fanny, one suspects, had already lost her heart to Captain Fuller, whom she describes as possessing 'figure, understanding, education, vivacity and intelligence' and she loved the way that, although only 21, he appeared to treat his company as would the father of a family of nice but naughty children—but surely she had been treated to an unusual glimpse of eighteenth-century military life?

It stands out in contrast, for instance, with the gruesome incident a few years later when some soldiers of the Oxford Militia who were stationed at East Blatchington demonstrated against the meagreness of their rations by breaking into the local mill and throwing a cargo of corn into the river. Two of the soldiers were sentenced to death by firing squad and five others to 300 lashes each, and so great was the tension that 13 infantry regiments had to stand guard, along with the artillery and the cavalry, when the sentences were carried out at Hove, to prevent any possible mutiny. (The British army, incidentally, was said to use 6,500 tons of flour a year at this period for the powdering of wigs.)

Meanwhile Miss Burney had a good time in Brighton; and on the last morning of their stay she and her friends got up at six o'clock for a final dip. 'By the pale blink of the moon we went to the sea-side, where we had bespoke the bathing-women to be ready for us, and into the ocean we plunged. It was cold but pleasant . . . We then returned home by candle-light, and as soon as we could get Dr Johnson ready, we set out upon our journey in a coach and chaise, and arrived at Argyle Street at dinner time.'

CHAPTER 5

Enter the Prince of Wales

Born in a period of ruffles and diamond-hilted swords that were not infrequently used, George Augustus Frederick (whose antics as Prince of Wales, Regent and King have been such a godsend to novelists and TV producers, if not to his contemporaries) lived to see a cluster of top-hatted gentlemen travelling on a railway train. His friend Creevey thought the locomotive machine was 'a lark of a very high order'[1] whereas Lord Sefton was convinced that 'some damnable thing must come of it'. Be that as it may, Prinny's life opened in an age of aristocracy and concluded with the triumph of steam.

A formidable transition to be sure. Yet midway between the classical movement of the eighteenth century and the romantic movement of the nineteenth, between Dr Johnson and Wordsworth, between the Age of Reason and the First Reform Bill, came that charming, eccentric, sentimental, extravagant and rather racy era which is associated with the Prince Regent. He saw umbrellas replace swords (they were carried, to Wellington's disgust, by officers in the Peninsular War) and velvet or brocade give way to morning coats and pantaloons. The French had their Revolution; Napoleon was defeated; America was lost; the old world of the land-owning gentry was overtaken by the new world of puffing billies. And Brighton became the sanctum of Royalty.

10. The Prince of Wales depicted when he was still a slim and handsome young man. His first love 'Perdita' recalled 'the grace of his person, the irresistible sweetness of his smile, the tenderness of his melodious but manly voice'.

1. In 1829 they travelled five miles at a speed of 23 m.p.h., which Creevey considered frightful. 'It is really flying,' he wrote, 'and it is impossible to divest yourself of the notion of instant death to all upon the least accident happening. It gave me a headache which has not left me yet.'

Certainly the 1780s were a rumbustious time. 'Perhaps no set of men and women since the world began enjoyed so many different sides of life, with so much zest, as the English upper class at this period,' says Trevelyan. 'Humanities' was the key word, observes T.H. White, pointing out how astonishingly well-educated this upper class had become. So effectively had the classics been thrashed into its members that Latin poets were quoted freely in conversation and Greek tags were heard in the House of Commons. Fox was an authority on Cassandra of Lycophron; Horace Walpole could print a fine edition or write about Richard III. Society went nightly to hear Handel or the Opera in London (and filled the New Theatre in Brighton); George III was found reading Paine's *The Rights of Man* in a bookshop at Windsor. Even the scandalous John Wilkes, who belonged to the Hellfire Club before setting Parliament by the ears, sat quietly editing Theophrastus during his visits to Brighton.

Though the Prince of Wales' education covered religion, morals, government and laws, mathematics and natural philosophy, history and 'polite literature', the classics were drummed into him too. He was taught to translate Homer as well as construe Latin; to cultivate a taste for the arts in addition to understanding Euclid. His upbringing at Kew was strict and teutonic. George III shared a firm belief in the value of corporal punishment. (Whenever the King crossed the river from Windsor Castle to Eton, he would rein his horse and shout jovially at its scions: 'Well, well, well my boy! When were you flogged last, eh, eh? Put him on the bill, Praeposter; he must be flogged.') And he practised on his own sons what he preached for others. Princess Amelia remembered seeing her brothers 'held by their tutor and flogged like a dog with a long whip'.

This rigorous training made him the best educated if not the best brought up of our Princes. By early manhood he was accomplished but rebellious, ready to burst out of his father's dull cheese-paring court like an obstreperous child from school. It was all very well to roister around fashionable London with a set of loose-living cronies, such as the actor John Philip Kemble who 'swallowed wine by the pailfull'; or Richard Cosway, the miniaturist, who was said to have turned his house into a brothel; or Sir John Lade, whose wife Lettie had been the mistress of 'Sixteen-string Jack' the highwayman; or George Hanger, 'The Knight of the Black Diamond', a beautifully powdered dandy who was in perpetual hiding from his creditors. But to be constantly in the company of notorious drunkards such as the ninth Duke of Norfolk and the fourth Duke of Queensbury, both many years his senior, was bound to excite unfavourable comment. Almost every day there were reports of his wild behaviour, of drunken brawls at Vauxhall, at Ranelagh, or at Lord Chesterfield's house at Blackheath. Moreover, in the words of a contemporary biographer, he was 'continually seen in those pavilions of Pleasure, where honour is not known, and female virtue for ever vanished', and gossips spoke of his successful conquests of easily conquered ladies.

At the age of 17, after several romantic assignations within the royal household, he fell passionately in love with the actress Mary Robinson, who was appearing at Drury Lane in *The Winter's Tale*. Playing Florizel to her Perdita, he persuaded her to become his mistress with a promise of £20,000—which he subsequently repudiated once he got bored with her, though the King had to pay £5,000 and an annuity of £500 to recover his compromising letters. [2]

The cartoonists, of course, had a field day. Lampoons of Perdita and Florizel were still displayed in shop windows when the Prince transferred his affections to Mrs Grace Dalrymple Elliot, the divorced wife of a rich physician. She was swiftly followed by brief attachments to Lady Augusta Campbell, the flirtatious daughter of the Duke of Argyll; Lady Melbourne, the mother of Queen Victoria's prime minister; and the brash scheming Countess von Hardenburg, to name but a few. Yet significantly these liaisons all conformed to a pattern he was to follow for the rest of his life: that of choosing more experienced married women who were a few years older than himself.

Cultivated, witty and floridly handsome, the Prince charmed everyone he met. Men found his charm fascinating, women scarcely resistible. Yet in truth he was probably less of an insatiable Don Juan given to erotic adventures than a rather insecure man looking for stability in a cosy, sentimental, and perhaps platonic companionship with older women. The Mother image!

Furthermore he exasperated his father by his increasing intimacy with three remarkable Whigs: Edmund Burke, who favoured Catholic emancipation; Charles James Fox, who opposed the Royal Marriage Bill and was in sympathy with the American colonists; and Richard Brinsley Sheridan, the brilliant and versatile playwright. It was not just that these men were politically unacceptable to the King. Like so many of the Prince's friends, Fox was a compulsive gambler, Sheridan more times than not drunk. With such a pair of wild spendthrifts keeping him company night after night, the young Prince was hardly likely to follow his father's frugal habits. He was soon heavily in debt, and never really got out of it.

Worse still, in the King's opinion, were his uncles. The Duke of Gloucester had been banished from court when it came out that he had been secretly married for five years to the illegitimate daughter of a well-known Whig. And in 1770 damages of £10,000 were awarded against the Duke of Cumberland for having seduced the wife of Lord Grosvenor. There followed the Duke's affair with a woman named Olive Wilmot, whose daughter insisted on calling herself Princess Olive of Cumberland. And hardly was this over than the Duke began lavishing his affection on Andrew Horton's frolicksome spouse. 'It was uncertain' commented Horace Walpole, 'which was most proud of the honour, husband or wife.' But as Mr Horton conveniently died, the question did not arise for long: and while honeymooning in Calais the Duke wrote to inform the King of his clandestine marriage. A direct result of these unions was the Royal Marriage Act of 1772, which was later to cause so much trouble for the Prince of Wales. [3]

2. Having collected the money, Mrs Robinson left for Paris, where she became involved with the Duc d'Orleans. This liaison cannot have been successful, for she returned to Brighton and wrote a pitiful letter to the Prince from the Old Ship informing him of her straitened circumstances. Luckily, however, while she was there she met the Member of Parliament for Liverpool, whose mistress she became for the next 16 years.

3. By this piece of legislation none of the descendants of George II (save those of foreign birth) could marry under the age of 25 without the King's consent.

Like so many of the Hanoverians, the Duke of Cumberland was a boorish profligate who took a perverse pleasure in doing all the thing most likely to annoy his long-suffering brother. He cultivated the society of opposition Whigs, ran a lavish string of race horses, and encouraged high play and heavy drinking at Cumberland House. His style of life was such an exhilarating contrast to the depressing routine at Windsor and Kew that it could hardly fail to appeal to the impressionable Prince of Wales, himself smarting from parental disapproval. And his uncle was only too happy to lead young 'Taffy', as he called him, still further astray.

In 1779 the Cumberlands rented Dr Russell's old house at the south end of the Steine, and immediately began whipping up the pace in Brighton. Most people were delighted to find themselves rubbing shoulders with members of the Royal family, even if the Duke drank them under the table and the Duchess' conversation was not noticeably refined—she was a coquette beyond measure, thought Horace Walpole, 'with the most amorous eyes in the world and eyelashes a yard long'. But staider folk had misgivings. 'This place is as full as an egg' commented the *Morning Herald* in September 1782. 'But the company is a motley group. The Duke is at the head of the whole and condescendingly associates with all from the baron to the blackleg—play runs high, particularly at Whist. We have every kind of amusement that fancy can desire for the train of folly and dissipation.'

There was nothing that the Prince of Wales would have liked better than to take part in these lively pleasures. But though unable to prevent nephew and uncle from meeting in London, the King could stop his son from going to Brighton. Since the occasion when the Prince had cut one of His Majesty's levées to go hunting in Northamptonshire, he had been forbidden to travel more than 50 miles from London, and Brighton was just outside the limit. It is said that the boundary stones were moved a couple of miles inland, and it has even been suggested that Reigate viaduct was dug to beat this ban. But whatever the truth in such tales may be, there is no record of any visit by the Prince before he attained his majority. Horace Walpole says that he told his uncle: 'I cannot come to see you now without the King's leave; but in three years I shall be of age, and then I may act for myself. I declare I will visit you.'

'And he kept his word,' observes Sir Osbert Sitwell. 'Brighton's great day had dawned and, as if to herald it, as if in imitation of more primitive days, when the tribe would assuredly have made some sacrifice to the God of Fortune, now arrived in the guise of the young Prince, the life of a young man was offered up.'

Or, in the more prosaic words of the *Sussex Weekly Advertiser*: 'At half past six on September 7th [1783] his Royal Highness's arrival was announced by the ringing of bells and a royal salute of guns at the battery when unhappily, through some indiscretion in reloading one of the pieces, it went off and wounded the under-gunner mortally. His body was blown off the battery to some distance on the beach.'

After this unfortunate start, everything went splendidly. The Prince and the Duke strolled together for half an hour on the Steine, and put in an appearance at the Assembly Rooms before 'the brilliancy of the evening concluded by a grand display of fireworks in front of the Duke's house'.

By now the Cumberlands had moved to a redbrick mansion overlooking

11. *The Promenade Grove was opened in 1793 as a pleasure garden and the Prince of Wales and his friends were frequent visitors. It occupied the centre of what is now the Western Lawn of the Royal Pavilion. On 12 August 1795 the Prince's birthday was celebrated at the Promenade Grove by the most dazzling display of fireworks ever seen at Brighton*

the Steine and Promenade Grove, where the music room of the Royal Pavilion now stands. The Prince stayed with them at Grove House for eleven days, his activities eagerly followed by both populace and press. He rode with the stag hounds (rising in his stirrups, it was noted, in the new English style). He had a plunge in the sea; he danced a minuet at the Old Ship and the Castle, went twice to the Theatre (causing an overflow each time of some 200 persons); and ended up at a ball that was described as the most splendid that Brighton had ever seen.

Very jolly and relaxed it all was. For instance, when the Hon. Tommy Onslow had the misfortune to clout a gatepost as he turned his gig into Grove House, the Prince and the Duke, who were watching from a window, poked such fun at him that Onslow, who was one of the most skilful drivers of the day, retaliated by betting them ten guineas each that he would gallop his four-in-hand 20 times through both gateways without touching. Whereupon the horses were immediately put-to, and Onslow emerged twenty guineas the richer 'by performing the task with great ease and dexterity'.

If the Prince loved Brighton and found the company of his raffish uncle more congenial than that of his censorious father, Brighton was enchanted by the Prince. People liked the smile that constantly broke out from his handsome if slightly sulky face; they were won over by his elegant and amiable demeanour. True the Duchess of Devonshire, who had taught him the graceful manners of the *vieille cour*, was a trifle more critical. His figure, she thought, though striking, was by no means perfect. 'He is inclined to be too fat and looks too much like a woman in men's cloaths' she observed. 'But the gracefulness of his manner and his height certainly make him a pleasing figure. His face is very handsome and he is fond of dress even to a tawdry degree.'

Here in Brighton he sported the fashionable Macaroni style that Brummell was later to deplore: exquisitely-cut embroidered silk coats ablaze with French paste buttons; laced cocked hats embellished with steel beads. Whether attired in a bottle-green coat and claret striped breeches, set off by

45

a silver tissue waistcoat, or in immaculate white nankeens when on horse-back, he seemed everything that a Prince should be: tall, resplendent and witty, a stylish dancer in the ballroom, with a good seat on a horse—both necessary articles for acceptance in those days.

He left telling everyone he would be back, and sure enough the following July word went round that the porcine little man enquiring for a house in unintelligible Anglo-German jargon was in fact the Prince's chef. As the *Sussex Weekly Advertiser* soon divulged, 'Mr Weltje, Clerk of the Prince of Wales's Kitchen' had been in Brighton to 'engage a house there for His Royal Highness, who has been advised by his physicians to sea-bathing, as necessary to Perfect the reestablishment of his health'.

The house that Weltje chose—he was often employed by his royal master in operations of a more delicate nature than just cooking—was located on the west side of the Steine, next door to that belonging to the Duke of Marlborough. It was leased from Thomas Kemp, the Member of Parliament for Lewes, whose son was later to give his name to Kemp Town, and was described by Samuel Rogers (who dined there as a boy) as being 'a respectable farmhouse'. Yet this was the genesis of the Royal Pavilion.

The Prince drove himself down from London in a new type of phaeton called a 'randem', drawn by three horses one before the other. He arrived too late for the welcoming celebrations, and slipped into the theatre without being recognised by the audience. Clearly there was something on his mind. For only three days later, anticipating the modern commuter, he made his famous ride to London and back, leaving Brighton on horseback at five in the morning and returning the same day. 108 miles in ten hours! No wonder he skipped the ball that was being given in his honour, and went exhausted to bed.

It is tempting to speculate on the reason for this dramatic dash. A biographer once suggested that it was neither the health-giving properties of the sea air, nor even the marine views that drew the Prince to Brighton, but rather 'the angelic figure of a sea-nymph whom he one day encountered on one of the groins of the beach'. Which was nonsense. Despite her charms, so vividly commemorated by Rex Whistler's painting, poor delicious but ignorant Charlotte Fortescue, for whom the Prince did have a brief moment of passion that summer, hardly stood a chance. (He dropped her immediately, what's more, when he found out that she was also having an affair with his friend George Hanger.)

The fact is that by now his heart was irrevocably set on a lady who, a couple of years earlier, could have been seen sitting in the drawing room of the Old Ship Hotel, or occasionally promenading on the Steine. Dressed in the deepest mourning, although she was only in her 25th year, this charming young woman with her pleasantly rounded figure, clear skin and golden hair, could hardly pass unnoticed in the frivolous crowds. But that, to be sure, was before the Prince ever set foot in Brighton. And now she was no longer there, but in London.

One of the most famous love stories in history was beginning. Perhaps that was why he rode so furiously?

CHAPTER 6
Mrs Fitzherbert

The solitary lady at the Old Ship had twice been bereaved. Her first husband had fallen off a horse and broken his neck, leaving her a widow at 18. The second had died of a chill caught while trying to restrain a violent mob in the Anti-Popery riots.

Sometimes, as her dark hazel eyes roamed over the seascape, or as she entertained a few intimate friends at her home in Twickenham—a lovely Palladian house built by George II for Henrietta Howard—it had seemed that life could hold no further joys or sorrows. But gradually this doleful mood passed, and she moved to a house she had inherited in Park Street. In March 1784 the *Morning Herald* announced: 'Mrs Fitzherbert is arrived in London for the season.'

A few days later, as she was leaving the Opera with her uncle, Henry Errington, the Prince came up unceremoniously with the flattering words: 'Who the devil is that pretty girl you have on your arm, Henry?'

From then on he pursued her feverishly. He made no secret of his feelings: Lord Wentworth was told by his sister that the Prince was 'making fierce love to the widow Fitzherbert' and that he looked like succeeding. But though gratified by his attentions, she gave him no encouragement. Indeed, says her biographer, she 'resisted with the utmost anxiety the flattering assiduities of the most accomplished Prince of his age'.

Her restraint was understandable, for she came from an old, if impoverished, Catholic family and had been strictly brought up at a convent in Paris. As a devout Roman Catholic, there could be no question

12. Maria Fitzherbert and George, Prince of Wales were married secretly on 15 December 1785. Although his life was punctuated with affairs and he made a disastrous marriage with Caroline of Brunswick, the Prince retained his affection for Maria, though separated from her for many years. On his deathbed it was discovered that he wore a miniature of Maria and this was buried with him at Windsor

of her becoming his mistress; nor, because of her religion, could she marry him. The King would never consent to the marriage of a Catholic with the heir to the throne. Yet the more she resisted the more hysterical he grew. Since she refused to become his mistress, he became determined to marry her, despite all the provisions of the Royal Marriage Act. He was ready to forfeit his rights to the throne; he threatened to commit suicide if she turned him down.

By July she had decided to go into hiding. But before she could do so, four members of the Prince's Household arrived at her house 'in the utmost consternation' to tell her that he had stabbed himself and only her immediate presence could save him. At first, fearing a trap, she refused. Only their insistence that his life was in real danger persuaded her to change her mind, provided that the Duchess of Devonshire went with her as chaperone.

They found the Prince lying covered in blood with a glass of brandy by his side. No one was sure what had happened and we shall probably never know either. The Prince said he had stabbed himself with a sword; though it was rumoured that after being blooded to relieve his feverish tension, he had torn off the bandage and smeared the blood over his chest. Be this as it may, poor Mrs Fitzherbert was so overcome by the sight that when assured that 'nothing would induce him to live unless she promised to become his wife', she meekly permitted him to take a ring from the Duchess' finger and put it on her own.

But once back home she felt that she had been the victim of a *coup monté* and determined to go abroad until the Prince's infatuation had subsided. Doubtless he had been in earnest—afterwards she said that she had frequently seen the scar. But she considered that 'promises obtained in such a manner are entirely void'. A few days later, accompanied by Lady Anne Lindsay, she sailed for France and after travelling around Europe eventually settled at Plombières in the Vosges.

It may well be that the Prince had wind of her plans when he rode so furiously from Brighton. Certainly he would have followed her to France had the King not refused his permission to go abroad on account of the Prince's mounting expenses—though his father must have known that his reason for leaving the country was love and not money. Instead, he pursued her with such a flow of impassioned letters that a political plot was suspected, and some of the couriers arrested. Beside himself with frustrated passion—according to Lord Holland, he cried by the hour and rolled about on the floor—he wrote epistles 40 pages long offering to renounce the throne and take her off to America.

After more than a year, tired of her self-imposed exile and reassured, perhaps, by reports that the Prince was being pressed by his family to become betrothed to Princess Louise of Orange, Mrs Fitzherbert returned to England, only to find that he was still just as impassioned and more determined than ever to marry her. And so at last she gave in, on the understanding that the marriage would be secret.

To find an Anglican parson willing to officiate at what was, in fact, a felony, proved no easy matter. But eventually a young curate, who was incarcerated in Fleet Prison for debt, agreed to perform the service, in return for the discharge of his debts and the promise of a bishopric when the Prince became King.

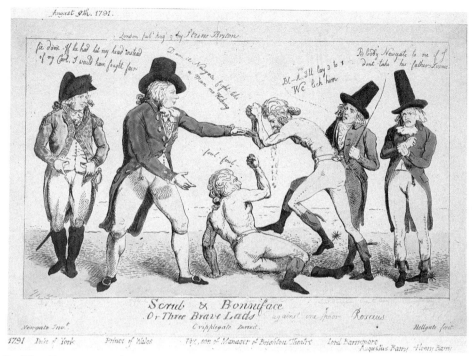

6. The Barrymore brothers

7. The Court at Brighton à la Chinese

8. The Great Joss and his Playthings

9. By Royal Authority – a new way of mounting a horse

So at dusk on 15 December 1785 the Prince slipped into Mrs Fitzherbert's house, where the ceremony was conducted in the drawing room behind locked doors. A certificate of marriage, made out in the Prince's hand (and now preserved at Coutts' Bank) was handed to her, and the pair left for a brief honeymoon in Richmond. But inevitably the news began to spread. Though the Prince denied it, several people knew that the wedding had taken place and many others believed the rumours which were circulating; Gilroy's caricature 'Wife or no wife' was discussed in every coffee-house. It was true, people said, that they lived in different houses, but they were virtually inseparable. Where the Prince went, Mrs Fitzherbert had to be asked also, and be placed at his table. Except at Court, they were received as man and wife.

Yet this ambiguous affair was overshadowed by a growing row over the Prince's debts which were discovered to have reached more than £250,000—over five times his official allowance, and probably a hundred times more in our deflated currency. (Imagine spending £2,500, the modern equivalent of his weekly expenditure on hair lotions and soap alone!)

Faced with this staggering figure, the long-suffering monarch refused to come to his son's aid unless he saw 'a prospect of reasonable security against a continuance of such extravagance'. Amid all the official huffing and puffing it was hinted that his father would prove more amenable if the Prince agreed to marry some suitable foreign princess, and abandon his open support of the Whig opposition. Both of which things the Prince refused vehemently to do. Instead he made a dramatic gesture. Announcing that he would shut up Carlton House, dismiss most of his Household, sell his horses and carriages, and not appear again in public until he could so with 'that dignity and splendour' to which he was entitled, he departed, in the words of the *Morning Post*, as 'an outside passenger on the Brighton Dilly', leaving Mrs Fitzherbert to follow him down to the coast a fortnight later.

Except for the King, who felt that his son was flaunting his poverty, most people applauded the Prince's decision to economise. And indeed that summer he spent very quietly in his little farmhouse at Brighton. It was a singularly pretty picturesque cottage, his biographer Cory tells us, surrounded by a small rose-garden that shut out the road but not the view of the sea. With Mrs Fitzherbert installed in a villa nearby, the two of them were happy alone with only a few friends like Sheridan, George Hanger and Sir John Lade to keep them in touch with London and liven things up. The story of the military gentleman, mounted by 'a jockey, booted and spurred', racing a fat bullock across the Steine sounds like one of their pranks. But otherwise the Prince, though still only 24, passed the time as sedately as any retired gentleman on holiday with his beloved—who was thought to be pregnant.[1] He rode on the Downs, walked unattended on the Steine, and of an evening could be seen drinking tea with the rest of the company at the Old Ship or the Castle. He engaged a bathing machine too, and once, having swum out further than the dipper, 'Smoaker' Miles, thought prudent, was pulled back to shore by the ear. 'I aren't ago'en to let the King

1. Mrs Fitzherbert never denied having had children, and the niece she adopted is believed to have been in reality her daughter by the Prince.

13. *It is fitting that this delicate portrait of Maria Fitzherbert was painted by Richard Cosway who had been appointed painter-in-ordinary by the Prince of Wales himself. The painting was engraved by Condé and published in 1792 three years before the Prince's ill-fated marriage to Princess Caroline of Brunswick*

hang me' growled Smoaker, 'for letten the Prince of Wales drown hisself, not I, to please nobody, I can tell 'e.' The Prince, whose ears were a prominent feature at the best of times, was so amused by the incident that he engaged 'Smoaker' permanently, and later rewarded him with a pension.

But the novelty of economising soon wore thin, and it was fortunate that Sheridan was able to hoodwink Parliament so brilliantly on his behalf the following spring, thus resolving both *l'affaire Fitzherbert* and the settlement of his debts. With these paid off and his income increased, he immediately commissioned Henry Holland, who was working for him on Carlton House in London, to restructure and enlarge his property on the Steine. The little farmhouse was incorporated into a far more imposing structure, which 150 craftsmen and labourers erected with remarkable speed.

The Marine Pavilion, as it was then called, emerged as a cream-coloured Palladian villa. E-shaped in plan, it centred around a semi-circular portico

of six Ionic columns surmounted by statues and a small recessed dome. Inside, the corridors were painted blue, the dining room yellow and maroon with a pale blue ceiling. The library was 'fitted up in the French style', and the Prince's bedroom in the southern wing was hung with quilted chintz. By means of judiciously-placed looking glasses he could enjoy an extensive view of the sea and the Steine while lying behind the green and white silk curtains draped like a tent around his bed. And though the Prince insisted that he was 'not a gaming man' the billiards room was fitted out with 'hazard, billiards and money tables'. In striking contrast, moreover, to most English houses, the whole building was powerfully overheated. One evening Sheridan asked George Hanger if he did not feel hot. 'Hot as hell' exclaimed Hanger. 'It is well that we should be prepared in this world for what we know will be our lot in another!' was the playwright's response.

Outside, the citizens watched these developments with proud excitement, conscious that Brighton was reaching a peak. Indeed, the arrival of the Prince of Wales was the focal point of its history. Sitwell called him Brighton's 'Patron Saint'. But if Prinny was hardly a saint (though, as Antony Dale reminds us, the Prince's portrait by Lawrence, sent as a gift to Pope Pius VII, was used as an altar-piece in the Church of St John Lateran in Rome until the mistake was pointed out) unquestionably he was a patron who brought a spirit of panache and dazzle to the town. As members of the

14. Thomas Rowlandson painted this scene of the Saloon at the Royal Pavilion. The Saloon was the centre of the original building and it was where the Prince began to experiment with the Oriental taste by having panels of Chinese wallpaper. The social life at the Pavilion was sparkling but many visitors found the heat of the rooms overpowering

fashionable world hurried to follow the Prince's example by building or acquiring dwellings of their own, Brighton speedily turned into the liveliest, most elegant place not only in England, but in the whole of Europe.

That year two rows of houses, the North and South Parades, were erected on the east of the Steine by supporters of the Prince and Charles James Fox (who painted them in blue and buff Whig colours). Others followed along the Marine Parade and in streets running north from the sea, so that within a few years the number of dwellings had doubled. Moreover, the town began to take on the character of a Whig stronghold—when Pitt appeared on a visit it was immediately assumed that he had come down to propose a coalition with Fox—though in reality the society that gathered around the Prince was more intent on pleasure than politics.

True, this society was not all made up of aristocratic *ton*. Once it became known that the Prince intended to live in Brighton, the town became the headquarters of half the scoundrels in the South of England. Blue-blooded Grandes Dames (themselves perhaps parvenues a generation or two back) glanced frigidly at the demi-reps and vulgarians who turned up in their hundreds—indeed Sitwell, neatly transposing the word Brighton for Bath in Smollett's denunciation of that resort, thought it even more true of Brighton now. '"Every upstart of fortune, harnessed in the trappings of the mode, presents himself in Brighton, as the very focus of observation" complains Matthew Bramble snobbishly in *Humphrey Clinker*. "Clerks and factors from the East Indies, loaded with the spoils of plundered provinces . . . hucksters from our American plantations . . . commissaries and contractors who have fattened in two successive wars . . . usurers, robbers and brokers of every kind, men of low birth and no breeding . . . discharge their wealth without taste or conduct, through every channel of the most absurd extravagance; and all of them hurry to Brighton, because here, without any further qualification, they can mingle with the princes and nobles of the land."'

The Prince had plenty of raffish friends himself, whose qualification for admittance to the Pavilion was the ability to amuse its owner. Most of these young reprobates were Irish and connected with the Turf, for the Prince was fascinated by horses and carriages. It is said that when he offered to call on the Lord Chancellor who was laid up with gout in his house on the cliff, Lord Thurlow replied gruffly that he would be honoured by a visit, 'But his Royal Highness must leave his scum behind him.' And on hearing that Lade was to be a fellow guest at the Pavilion, Thurlow growled: 'I have no objection to Sir John Lade in his proper place, but that I take to be your Royal Highness's coach-box, and not your table.'

Thurlow may have been a politician of more duplicity than most politicians. (When lying to the House he would speak 'in a state of agitation which continued till a flood of tears came to his relief'.) But he had some justification for these rebukes. Though a nephew of the learned Mrs Thrale, Sir John was impenetrably stupid about everything save horses, while his wife's vocabulary was so scurrilous that the Prince would say of anyone who was unusually foul-mouthed that 'he swears like Lettie Lade'. (Alas, the poor soul ended up as a pickpocket in Augsburg, where she was sentenced to clean the streets, chained to a wheel-barrow.)

What's more the Prince and his entourage had a passion for practical jokes. No one was safe from them, not even himself, One night he was given the fright of his life when he woke up to find a donkey with a pair of horns and festooned with firecrackers peering into his bed; another time Lord Barrymore dressed up as a woman and sang 'Ma chère amie' under the windows of Mrs Fitzherbert's house to the accompaniment of a guitar at three in the morning.

Yet if the Prince was sometimes the victim of crude jokes, he was fond of horseplay himself. An excellent shot, he merrily sniped at the chimney pots of neighbouring houses when shooting doves on the Steine. And one day, when happening to go into the Pavilion kitchen, he came across Martha Gunn the dipper, who was a great favourite with the staff. The cook, it seems, had given Martha a pound of butter. Spotting her slip it surreptitiously into her pocket, the Prince manouevred her nearer and nearer to the great kitchen fire as he talked, until the butter melted down her clothes and formed a pool on the floor. Then, laughing heartily, he retired.

Another time his butt was Admiral Sir Edmund Nagle, a weather-beaten sailor who commanded the Brighton Sea Fencibles, often from his table in the corner of the Old Ship's dining room. (The stout boots of the Brighton fishermen, said *The Times*, armed with swords and pikes, 'could be transformed into a formidable flotilla on the first appearance of danger'. But the admiral's private joke was that the Brighton hoteliers, armed with their *Bills*, would have scattered the enemy with their first *charge*.)

And, since there was nothing he fancied more than the Prince's cream-coloured Hanoverian horses, the old sea-dog was overjoyed to be presented with what was apparently an animal from the Royal Stud. Only later, when caught in the rain, did he find himself riding a piebald—his own horse, in fact, that had been daubed with a coat of white paint.

It is only fair to record that the Prince subsequently gave him the genuine article, just as he sent Martha Gunn back home with a new dress and enough victuals to keep her contented. Though he delighted in absurd pranks—once, draped in table-cloths and grotesque headdresses made of napkins, his dinner-guests swayed around the churchyard uttering mournful groans, to the distress of nervous ladies who lived in the vicinity—the Prince's own leg-pulls were tame and goodnatured compared with those of his friends.

Of these, the wildest were the Barrymore brothers. Reckless, insolvent, unprincipled (but never dull), they lived up to their nicknames: Richard, the seventh Earl, was known as 'Hellgate'; Henry, being club-footed, as 'Cripplegate'; and Augustus, the youngest, as 'Newgate', the only jail he had never served time in. (Their sister, Caroline, was called 'Billingsgate' because of her vocabulary.)

Even as boys the 'Barrys' were always up to mischief. They would go out at night and swap the sign posts of all the inns for miles around their home at Wargrave. When Richard came to Brighton at the age of 20, one of his favourite pastimes was to drive around the narrow lanes in a high phaeton, cracking bedroom windows to get a better view of the nocturnal activities within. 'Fanning the daylight', he called it. And at the Old Ship, dark stains on the walls of their sitting room showed where 'Hellgate' and 'Newgate' had hurled bottles of port at each other.

One night 'Cripplegate' rode his horse up to an attic in Mrs Fitzherbert's house. Unfortunately, having got there, the animal refused to turn tail, and eventually two blacksmiths had to be called in to help. Once they had finally succeeded in hauling it down, both the horse and its rescuers were rewarded with bowls of punch at the Old Ship, causing further stains on the floor. But Mrs Fitzherbert took the incident in good part. A day or two later she was out in her barouche, laughing at the antics of her coachman—the same young man dressed in a pink silk coat.

Some of the 'Barrys'' diversions were less amusing for the victims. That autumn they wrapped a dummy corpse in a shroud and fitted it into an open coffin. This they stood upright against a local worthy's front door in such a way that it would fall on the person who answered their knocking. The maid who opened the door fainted, and the tradesman's wife, who happened to be pregnant, was so terrified at what she took to be a corpse walking about in its coffin that she had a miscarriage.

Next, a live footman clothed in white, with a chalk-powdered face, was strapped into the coffin. This time the servant's shriek brought her master to the door, armed with a blunderbuss which he promptly discharged. The bullet missed the footman's head by less than an inch, and the wretched fellow was lucky to be able to disentangle himself and flee for dear life before the gun could be reloaded.

Not surprisingly, the brothers were united in their passion for the Turf. Richard ran several horses in the Brighton races, often riding himself. Being over six feet tall he was less suited to be a jockey than Sir John Lade, who lost no time in selling him a phaeton and eight greys for over £1,000. They were often to be seen on the Steine, performing feats of 'tooling' each other with their four- or six-in-hands. And after one of the Brighton meetings the two of them engaged in what they called an 'aquatic race', dashing into the sea with all their clothes on until the water reached their chins.

'O yonge fresshe folkes', as Chaucer would have said! After another meeting a French nobleman bet Sir Thomas Bunbury 20 guineas that he would run half the length of the Steine backwards in less time than Sir Thomas's nominee could run the whole distance forwards. A waiter from the Castle was summoned, and the pair began their race. It was a closely matched contest until someone shouted and the Frenchman stopped. But though he forfeited his stake, Bunbury sportingly refused to accept it.

It was around this time that Mr Wade, the MC, issued a warning from the Old Ship that any persons running 'any Foot or other Race, or Fight, Play Cricket, Trap, or any other Game' on the Steine would be prosecuted. This did not prevent arrangements from being made the following week for a 'grand Foot Race, for one hundred guineas, between Flint of Surrey and a Man from Kent', which caused much excitement in the town. Bets totalling more than £8,000 were deposited with John Hicks at the Old Ship, a stroke of policy, no doubt, given his influence with the MC. The race was run on each side of a rope stretched tight along the middle of the ground 'to prevent jockeying or foul play' and was won easily by the Kentish man, whose mother had thoughtfully sent him an empty purse to bring back full.

Enshrined, moreover, in Brighton lore is the story of how Bullock, the immensely fat owner of the Black Lion Brewery (along with a gaming establishment, some racehorses and a pawnshop) bet Lord Barrymore a large sum of money that he would beat him in a hundred yards sprint—on the understanding that he would be given 35 yards start, and could choose his own time and place.

Barrymore accepted without a thought. He knew he could do it on his head against a man who was so gross that he could hardly walk, let alone run. The Prince of Wales also laid a sizeable bet on what looked like a certainty.

But when the time came, it turned out that the venue chosen by Bullock was the narrow twitten between Black Lion Street and Ship Street, which still exists behind the Old Ship Hotel. And with his comfortable start the corpulent brewer was able to puff along, rolling from side to side in such a way that his huge frame filled the constricted space, and there was no way his opponent could get past him.

In another sly wager, George Hanger bet the Prince £500 that 20 geese would beat 20 turkeys in a ten mile race.

The Prince and his party set off with their turkeys, and after three hours were two miles or more ahead of the geese. But as dusk fell, the turkeys began to stretch out their necks towards the trees that lined the road. One by one, they flew up into the branches. Prodding them with a pole, or strewing barley on the ground proved equally useless. No stratagem could get them down from their roosting places.

In due course the geese came waddling along, and took the lead. But for the turkey party, no further progress was possible. In the words of Blake, a fool sees not the same tree that a wise man sees.

They'd been properly fooled.

CHAPTER 7
All is Pleasure

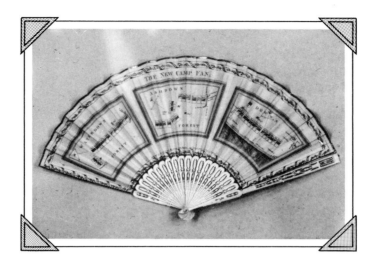

Now to Brighton all repair
To taste the pleasures that flow there
Sure no place was e'er like this:
All is pleasure, joy, and bliss.

Local doggerel, 1791

To the thousands of émigrés who began fleeing France in the autumn of 1789, this whimsical lighthearted place, so deliciously chic and *pas-sérieux*, must have seemed like a fable.

Of course many of the fashionable French were already familiar with Brighton, since it was just across the water and had almost the atmosphere of a continental city. Sportsmen like the Ducs de Chartres and de Lauzun, or the Marquis de Conflans, had been regular visitors at the Pavilion. Chartres—who became the Duc d'Orleans and subsequently, when titles were abolished, took the name of Philippe Egalité—had largely inspired the *anglomanie* that swept through Paris, causing young aristocrats to exchange their silk coats and lace ruffles for English hunting coats and riding boots, as they filled the capital with cockney grooms and London-built carriages. (Later, when the Duc carried his liberal opinions to the point of regicide, the Prince of Wales regretted his youthful friendship for this witty and charming man of the world—who was destined to end under the guillotine himself, leaving his son to fulfil his aspirations to kingship.)

Among the earliest fugitives to reach Brighton was Mrs Fitzherbert's

15. A souvenir fan of the 1790s depicting the famous Brighton Camp. Started originally as training manoeuvres in readiness for battle against the French, it quickly developed into a great social occasion as well. Young girls, as portrayed by Jane Austen's Lydia Bennet, thought Brighton comprised every possibility of earthly happiness mainly because of so many soldiers in dazzling scarlet. On the right of the fan, the design shows the disposition of the Camp at Brighton in 1793 after the soldiers had marched south from Ashdown Forest; St Nicholas's church is to the north east while to the south west, adjacent to the Hove boundary, is the Duke's pavilion, a very elaborate affair indeed

own cousin, the Marquise d'Osmond. She had managed to escape with her family from Versailles when the mob broke into the Palace. 'We landed at Brighton' recounts her daughter Adèle, 'and whom should my mother encounter—at the very moment of landing—but Mrs Fitzherbert, who happened to be strolling on the quay!' The little girl remembers being taken to the Prince's dressing room, where there was a huge table completely covered with shoe-buckles. 'I gave a cry of delight when I saw them, upon which Mrs Fitzherbert smilingly flung open a cabinet which was filled with as many more. The Prince had one for each day of the year!'

Since Dieppe was the nearest port to Paris, and Brighton lay directly across the Channel from Dieppe, the flood of refugees swelled as the reign of terror increased. For the same reason, invasion jitters returned when war with France broke out in 1793. Great tented camps sprang up on the Downs to accommodate thousands of regular soldiers and militia. These encampments spread from Belle Vue Field (now the site of Regency Square) westwards, and the continual parades and reviews, often graced by the Prince at the head of the 10th Light Dragoons, all added to the season's gaiety.

Enjoying himself enormously, Prinny invested these military functions with a pleasant lack of solemnity. At one review, a regiment of donkeys appeared. Mounted by 'beaux' and 'belles', they were led by the Prince, his spurs gleaming incongruously around the level of the hooves of his steed.

But sometimes things went amiss. Whenever manoeuvres were held on the Downs, they attracted spectators crammed into every kind of vehicle from barouches to fishcarts. One October morning, when the Prince (to quote *The Times*) was amusing the people with a sham fight, the defending troops, hotly pursued by an enemy shouting 'Victory!' were forced back into the crowd. Pandemonium ensued. Horses plunged, vehicles became hopelessly entangled with each other. Ladies shrieked, a child was trampled to death, and several people were badly hurt. It was a tragic affair, though had the battle been a real one, casualties would obviously have been far heavier.

Yet a real battle was what Brighton cheerfully anticipated, even if the nearest the French ever got was the report of an invasion received by Cavalry headquarters, which prompted the Colonel to mobilise his troops and charge down to the beach. There the fishermen and bathing women, imagining them to be the French invaders, went into action with broomsticks and fishnets, until it was discovered that the incident was just another of the Prince of Wales' jokes.

If his presence at Brighton was the principal reason for the town's popularity (and there is no doubt that it loved him, despite all his nonsense), the military camps also served to attract a large number of visitors. Summer after summer the place bristled with uniformed soldiers; and the appearance of so many elegant young Dragoons at the Assembly Rooms and on the Steine caused that flutter in female hearts which Jane Austen describes in *Pride and Prejudice*. Certainly it was the fascinations of 'the officers' that made Lydia Bennet persuade her parents to allow her to accept an invitation to the town from Colonel Forster's wife, whose kindness she repaid by eloping with the ineligible Wickham. 'In Lydia's imagination a visit to Brighton comprised every possibility of earthly happiness' Miss

Austen tells us. 'She saw, with the creative eye of fancy, the streets of that gay bathing place covered with officers. She saw herself the object of attention to tens and scores of them at present unknown. She saw all the glories of the camp—its tents stretched forth in beauteous uniformity of lines, crowded with the young and the gay, and dazzling with scarlet; and, to complete the view, she saw herself beneath a tent, tenderly flirting with at least six officers at once.' (These words, by the way, were written in 1796, though the novel was not published until some years later.)

The Brighton Camp inspired one of the most popular marching songs of the day, 'The Girl I left behind me'. It also attracted over three hundred prostitutes to the town, in addition to those in the Camp itself. ('Vivent l'Amour et Bacchus', commented *The Times*.) And it probably prompted John Hicks to inaugurate his famous breakfasts outside the Old Ship, which offered his guests the chance to witness spectacles no less exciting than those on the Downs. 'Nowadays,' says Musgrave, 'the sea offers little of interest compared to the days when the Brighton fleet numbered more than a hundred vessels, and its departure and return were a stirring sight . . . Sham sea-battles were fought, and from time to time the sight of a fleet of ships passing up-Channel, their white square sails and tall masts shining in the sun, would bring hundreds of people flocking to the beach.' And delight Hicks' patrons on the cliff-top, as they worked their way through devilled kidneys and a flagon of Madeira.

Clearly Hicks profited from the boom. In 1791 he extended his premises by buying two houses on the East Cliff to give the Old Ship considerably more sea-frontage. At one time, he owned nearly all the land stretching east from the Steine to Black Rock, and north to Preston parish boundary. This huge acreage, which today would be worth billions, included arable land as well as sheep down. Apart from the Old Ship, he had an interest in the Chailey and Cuckfield taverns, along with a share in the General Coach service that operated between Brighton and London.

In short, a man of substance. So it is surprising that he should have found himself in financial difficulties. No doubt he overreached himself with such diversification, and was often seriously strapped for cash—a frequent occurrence in those days, as the Prince and his friends discovered.

Be this as it may, Hicks took a mortgage of £1,500 on the Old Ship in 1774, and his mother also lent him £1,000. But by 1799 his affairs were in such a parlous state that the solicitor, William Attree, was called in to try and untangle the mess. It was all very complicated. For one thing, the mortgage on the Old Ship was not an entity, some parts of the property being leasehold. And there were other 'incombrances' on the tavern as well. Moreover, troubles emerged between mother and son. John Hicks was supposed to have made out a document conveying the Old Ship to her in guarantee for the money she had lent him, but had failed to do so. Consequently she hung on to other documents, and refused to give them to Attree. All in all, it sounds as though the solicitor deserved the fee of £1 0s 0d a day he charged for his many attendances on the pair of them. Yet as a matter of fact, he did better than that.

For in the middle of all the trouble, John Hicks solved his problems by dying. After the funeral Attree came to the Old Ship to read his will (for which he charged 13s 4d), and eight days later, on 11 April 1801, a

16. *The cover of the catalogue relating to the sale of the Old Ship and its contents in 1802. The auction was conducted by John Weller who had married the eldest Hicks daughter, the previous owner of the Old Ship. Not long after the auction Weller was waylaid by a footpad on the Portsmouth to Chichester road. Fortunately his wife had deposited £50 and his watch in a bank before he set out so he only lost his loose change*

17. *The original front of the Old Ship Tavern which was situated in Ship Street—the King's Road entrance was a later addition. The stabling for coach and horses was through the archway at the back of the premises. The Old Ship garage later occupied the old stable quarters*

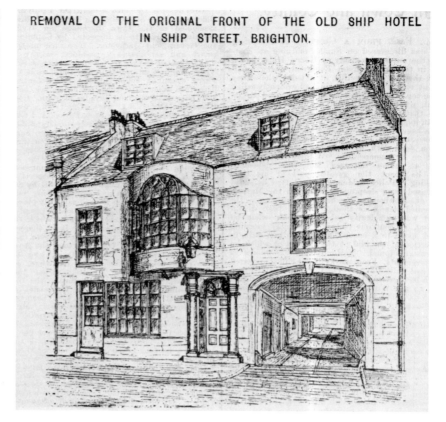

REMOVAL OF THE ORIGINAL FRONT OF THE OLD SHIP HOTEL IN SHIP STREET, BRIGHTON.

complete inventory of the contents of the Inn was made. This catalogue, which recently turned up among a batch of documents deposited at the East Sussex Record Office, shows that the Old Ship then had 70 beds, and also gives a fair idea of the standard of home comforts that it offered. For instance, there were goosefeather beds and quilts, pots de chambre in the bedrooms, and an impressive array of copper pans, coffee-pots, brass skillets, roasting jacks and spits in the kitchens. But neither tavern nor contents were disposed of until November 1802, by which time John Hicks' mother had also died. And when the Old Ship was then sold by auction, the successful bidder was none other than William Attree.

At this period there were no less than 41 inns and public houses in the town, a ratio of about one to every 30 private dwellings. The Seven Stars, the Ship in Distress, and the Star & Garter opposite the capstan used for hauling up boats, were favourite haunts of the fishing community. Then there were the Gun Tavern (now Harrison's Hotel) which was chiefly used for parish meetings; the Last & Fish Cart, renamed the Cricketers in 1790 when it became a gathering place for devotees of the game; the King & Queen, which provided for the agricultural community and operated a profitable sideline slipping liquor through a hole in the wall to soldiers in the barracks behind. All these were within a short distance of the Old Ship Hotel. The New Ship (now Henneky's) was just opposite. It was here that the Prince of Wales and Mrs Fitzherbert paid a surprise visit to 37 refugee nuns who had just arrived from France in 1789. Moving up to North Street, the New Inn was built as a coaching inn around 1785. Its name was changed to the Clarence Hotel when the Duke of Clarence succeeded to the throne as William IV, and its original severe façade remains almost unaltered today. Nor should one overlook the George in West Street—where Charles II spent the night before escaping to France—which was renamed the King's Head in about 1745, and became a watering hole for tradesmen. There was also the other George in Middle Street.

But the Castle and the Old Ship were still the leading hostelries, and the sly old solicitor knew what he was doing when he promptly leased his acquisition to Leonard Shuckard and Alexander Hicks, a son of the previous owner. In their capable hands the Old Ship thrived more than ever before. Gradually overtaking what had become its more prestigious competitor, it re-captured the patronage of most of the titled and wealthy visitors until in the end the Castle lost its former appeal.

Our chronicler J.G. Bishop confirms that the rivalry between the two establishments increased under the new management of the Old Ship. Assemblies were now held on the same evening at each of them, instead of being staggered as before. Instancing a ball held at the Castle in September 1808 which was opposed by a 'divertissement' at the Old Ship, he says that about 140 people attended the former against 500 at the latter. And Bishop quotes a contemporary publication which stated: 'The Castle, fronting the Steyne, and almost adjoining the Prince's Palace, has in no other point of view whatever the advantage of the situation of the Old Ship, which inn is more centrally situated in the town, in Ship Street, and though the rays of royalty but seldom irradiate the premises, the first families of nobility resort thither.'

Shergold's successors did their best to improve the Castle's facilities. But fashion was changing. The public's taste had drifted away from assemblies towards concerts and entertainments, which the Old Ship was quick to provide. Despite a rebuilding programme that gave the ballroom a new organ, the Castle's popularity sagged to such an extent that only 20 subscribers attended the inauguration of its redecorated premises, whereas over 500 guests flocked to the Master of Ceremonies' benefit ball held the same evening at the Old Ship.

No doubt Shuckard and Hicks were more successful with their public relations, and had Mr Wade's successor in their pocket. Certainly all the important town meetings, property sales and business gatherings were held at the Old Ship, which emerged as the unchallenged centre of activities throughout the Regency and for much of the reign of George IV.

But let us return to the Prince's salad days. Let us join Mr Bishop for a pipe or a dish of 'tay' among the fashionable crowd at the Old Ship, and take, in his own words, a 'peep into the past'. As editor of the *Brighton Herald* for over 40 years in the nineteenth century, he had access to the facts.

Loyal festivities (he begins by reminding us) had always been popular. 'They feasted the eye, gladdened the heart, gave scope for unrestricted hilarity', and had the advantage that everyone was free to join in. To celebrate Admiral Boscawen's victory in 1758 at Cape Breton, the official ball was supplemented by a great bonfire on the Steine, where the populace drank three hogsheads of ale in loyal 'healths'. Again, when George III and Queen Charlotte were crowned in October 1761, the ringing of bells and sermons in churches were enhanced by great quantities of beer.

But the tradition of loyal rejoicing really took root when the Prince of Wales' birthday was celebrated in Brighton for the first time, on 12 August 1789. 'The weather was heavenly. Grandeur and Elegance shook hands with Good Humour and Familiarity, and furnished a treat surpassing description for its blandishment and brilliancy.'

The celebrations began at midday when, amid a frenetic ringing of bells, the Prince, accompanied by the Duke of York, Mrs Fitzherbert and a party of friends, drove to a level space outside the town to watch the sports. These comprised 'Jack-ass racing, foot races by ladies for gowns, men running in sacks, etc.' A jingling match was won by a man called John Baker. 'Dressed up with bells, he escaped the pursuit of ten persons blindfolded for half an hour.' As prize, he received a jacket, a waistcoat and a laced hat. And there were plenty of other good-natured frolics to keep the spectators amused.

For the royal entourage, five marquees were provided. At a convenient distance from them, an ox was roasted for the townspeople. Mr Mercer, the Prince's butcher, carved the meat with a huge broadsword, and then dispensed it on the prongs of an enormous fork which served as a bayonet to keep the crowds at bay. Drink flowed. The gentry had their wine, and 20 hogsheads of strong beer satisfied the thirst of all comers. The fishermen took part in a sailing race for a set of sails as prize. In the evening the Prince gave a sumptuous reception for the local notabilities, while those who had not been invited to the Pavilion consoled themselves at a scarcely less magnificent ball at the Old Ship.

What is more, the birthdays of the Dukes of York and Clarence were celebrated if anything more lavishly just a week later. This time, in addition to the sports, there was 'dancing by young men and women' and a game of 'foot ball'. The Duke of York's side played cricket against Colonel Tarlston's team for 100 guineas, and lost. Two oxen, which had been roasting since five in the morning, were served at three o'clock in the afternoon by Mercer in full canonicals—that is, white coat and cap, with a broad sash of royal purple across his chest—and the vast quantities of ale provoked what were described as 'various feats in the arts of pugilism'. At night there were illuminations and a firework display.

These birthday celebrations became yearly events, often accompanied by exhibitions of fencing and boxing as well as a cricket match—and on at least one occasion a roughhouse when the Nottinghamshire militia made a concerted charge for the roast beef, which 'flew about in every direction'.

Of all the sporting contests, men and women's races were the most traditional. By 1746 Brighton already had its local champion who, so it seems, was only beaten by the Lewes man—for a wager of £40—because he was handicapped by having to carry a two pound weight in each hand.

Both walking matches and running marathons were then common. A gouty old alderman walked from Steyning to Findon for a wager; given $1\frac{1}{2}$ hours to cover the distance, he astonished everyone by doing it in an hour and five minutes. More seriously, large sums were bet on men's sprints. Students of Olympic form may be interested to learn that Grinley, the 'Brighton Boot-Closer', ran 140 yards in 13 seconds; while in 1806 Abraham Wood, a Lancashire lad, covered 20 miles in two hours $5\frac{1}{2}$ minutes. (After which he offered to run a further ten miles within the hour for any sum that might be put up.) Even greater excitement was aroused by his match with the celebrated pedestrian Captain Barclay, who was a frequent visitor to Brighton. For a prize of £200, each was to cover the greatest distance he could around the racecourse in 24 hours, the pedestrian being allowed a 20 mile start. Unhappily Wood had to give up after running 40 miles in six hours. But they were hardy souls in those days, for soon after this Barclay successfully accomplished the feat of walking 1,000 miles in 1,000 consecutive hours.

And they would do almost anything for a bet. When encamped at Brighton, Lieutenant Hooper of the South Gloucester Militia undertook to pick up 100 stones that were laid out at intervals of a yard, and deposit them one by one in a basket at the starting point within the period of an hour. This meant covering a distance of about $5\frac{3}{4}$ miles. He did it in $47\frac{1}{2}$ minutes. A fellow officer then bet he would do the same thing in 45 minutes, and performed the task with ten seconds to spare. 'Much money being won or lost', our chronicler adds. Another sporting gentleman wagered he would hop half a mile in 12 minutes on his right leg, without touching the ground with his left. He lost by a minute, to the 'no small disappointment of the knowing ones'.

Though women also competed, their participation in foot-races did not always meet with general approval. Before a women's race at Rottingdean, it had to be announced that 'the young women may depend on a Protection from any Insults from the Country People, as proper care will be taken by hiring persons for that purpose'. The fear of such disapproval may have weighed with the lady who challenged a gentleman to a race on the Steine for a ten guinea stake. When her offer was accepted, she went home 'to breech and otherwise equip herself for the conflict', but then failed to reappear.

Horse racing was even more popular. Lewes held meets early in the eighteenth century. Eastbourne and Steyning came next. Even Shoreham staged a two-day 'Open Meeting' in 1763. These events were eagerly followed by people in Brighton; the races at Lewes attracted a virtual exodus of both gentry and townsfolk. Such was the local interest that from 1774 onwards a 'Brighthelmstone Plate of £50' was raised by subscription and run on the last day of the Lewes meeting.

Finally subscribers decided that they should hold races at Brighton itself. A suitable site was chosen about a mile inland on the top of Whitehawk Hill. Here a group of sportsmen that included the Dukes of Cumberland and Queensbury, Lord Egremont, Lord George Cavendish, Sir Charles Bunbury and Sir Harry Featherstonehaugh of Uppark laid out a horseshoe-shaped course some two miles in length on the ridge of the down.

In August 1783 the first Brighton Races were run. Mr Adams' grey colt 'Puff' won the £50 Plate ahead of the favourite 'Adjutant'; and the pundits were again disappointed when Sir Charles Bunbury's mare 'Eliza' defeated Sir Ferdinand Poole's 'Diadem' in the best of three four-mile heats. Everyone was delighted with the new course, even though it had no stand, and the only way to see over the crowd was to be seated on horseback or in a carriage.

The Prince of Wales, attended by the Duc de Chartres, was present the following year, and from then onwards, the Races thrived under his

patronage. Both he and the Frenchman owned splendid racing studs. But though they entered horses for the 1785 Stakes, both paid forfeit; the nominations could not be taken up once the Prince's stable had been sold during his period of economising. However, his friends gambled heavily, and Fox lost his shirt.

In the meantime, a testy little incident occurred. By custom the owner of the land received a quarter of a pipe of wine every year for its use as a race-course, and when for some reason this failed to materialise, the farmer threatened to plough up his field unless he was given £100. Somewhat affronted, the Jockey Club refused. They made it clear that they would not be held up to ransom.

So the farmer set his ploughmen to work. He should have known, however, that the grandees of the racing world were more than a match for him. For hardly had a ridge or two been worked than the press-gang turned up. Whereupon the ploughmen all ran for their lives, and the races took place without further interruption. (Though whether the farmer ever got his wine is another matter.)

Cricket had been known since Stuart times in these parts. In 'Godwin's Rental' of 1665 mention was made of a bowling green on the Steine, and later there were references to cricket there too. By the early eighteenth century it was being played in most Sussex villages by both men and women. In 1743 we are told that 'noblemen, gentlemen and clergy were making butchers, cobblers or tinkers their companions' on the pitch, and in October 1752 a county match took place at Longdown between Sussex and Surrey, which Surrey won by 'about 4 score notches'. (The original method of scoring was by 'notches' on a stick.)

These encounters were played in the old style with two low stumps about a couple of feet apart and a third stump, or bail, laid across them. The space between the stumps was known as the 'popping hole', into which the batsman had to push his bat before the wicket-keeper could break his wicket by 'popping' the ball into it. The bat was shaped rather like a hockey stick and reached up to the height of one's elbow. Defensive batting was

10. The Royal Pavilion from the Steine

11. Great chandelier in the Banqueting Room

12. Roof of the port-cochère

unknown. 'The best batsmen were all hard hitters and had therefore a short and merry life of it,' observes our chronicler, 'while early bowlers were very swift, all along the ground and, of course, underhand.'

Brighton players are mentioned at Rottingdean in 1758. Ten years later, the Duke of Richmond's team took on the redoubtable Hambledon Club. Though the first game was lost, they won the return match and 'near £1,000' as well. But what might be called the Royal era of local cricket began around 1788, by which time the game had been radically altered. A third stump replaced the 'popping hole', and the height of the wicket was raised to 22 inches. Though indifferent players themselves, both the Prince of Wales and the Duke of York were fond of the game. Prinny endowed the 'Prince's Cricket Ground' in 1791, where one of the fixtures was between Brighton and Mary-Le-Bone. This match lasted four days and the home team won by three wickets.

It is pleasant to learn that when the young Comtesse de Noailles arrived in Brighton the following year—having escaped from France hidden for 14 hours on deck under a coil of rope—she was immediately taken by Mrs Fitzherbert to a cricket match. So her first impressions of these hospitable shores were those of watching Brighton beat Middlesex by five wickets 'for 500 guineas'. One wonders what she made of it all! But evidently the stakes were high in those days, for we hear of an encounter between the Earl of Winchelsea's team and a mainly local side which put 1,000 guineas in the Brightonians' pockets. And then of course there was the Duke of Queensbury's wager that he would have a letter conveyed by hand over a distance of 50 miles within an hour. 'Old Q' met the challenge by enclosing it in a cricket ball, which was then thrown from hand to hand by a team of expert cricketers.[1]

Another popular spectacle, so hallowed by time that it was said to have been brought over by the Romans, was cock-fighting. We know that Henry V built a pit at Whitehall; that James I went as often as twice a week, and that in the eighteenth century the cocks were in full feather, as they used to say, all over the country. Certainly battles took place at the Old Ship in 1746; perhaps even earlier than that. They were attended by what were euphemistically termed Gentlemen and Professional sporting men, who shrieked their bets around the little amphitheatre; and big money changed hands before a huge dinner was served. Later on, the Castle began to hold cock-battles too. But by the end of the century the White Lion seems to have taken over as the chief venue for this form of entertainment.

The even crueller practice of 'throwing at cocks' was also widespread. Tied to a post, the wretched bird was used as a mobile target at which to

1. Twenty-four of them were employed to do the job, Nimrod tells us, and successfully carried out the feat in under sixty minutes. Which—assuming the story to be true—says something for the skill of these early players, if they were able to throw a cricket ball over two miles, and catch it from the same distance too.

But toying over the implications of this episode at breakfast with Professor Geoffrey Blainey of Melbourne University, we increasingly wondered how it could possibly be true, since W.G. Grace was renowned as a strong-armed fielder and the best of his throws was 122 yards. And as the world record even in Bradman's day was only 140 yards 2 feet, it would have needed a line of more than 700 Graces, all in top form, to cover the 50 miles. It would have been possible for the Duke, had he time, to organise such a relay of cricketers; but the idea of a mere 24 beggars belief.

hurl stones. Sometimes it would be suspended in an earthern vessel for pot-shots. Four throws cost twopence, and if you were successful in breaking the pot, the cock was your prize. In fact there is no record of 'cock-shying' at Brighton, though it was a popular pastime at Lewes. But down on the beach until quite recently, boys used to throw pebbles at the effigy of a cockerel, which sounds like a vestige of the original custom.

From its early barnstorming days, the theatre has always been one of the most notable features in Brighton. And the first performances did indeed take place in a barn. They were given by a touring company, who had to ring down the curtain when the harvest was brought in from the cornfields (which came as no surprise to the players: their own theatre in Chichester was a malthouse, and at Southampton they performed in a silk-mill).

The barn was rigged up to form a pit; there were boxes and stalls round the sides, and a gallery up in the loft. The experiment must have been successful, for they returned in 1770 to stage a comic opera called *The Maid of the Milk* at the request of the Countess of Pembroke, and *The Clandestine Marriage* for Lady Masham. The Hon. Mrs Brudenel gave her patronage to a drama entitled *The Wonder*, and the last play to be performed was *The Merry Wives of Windsor*, apparently by the desire of Master and Miss Bathurst.

Four years later, a permanent theatre was built in North Street, by a bricklayer named Samuel Paine. A pretty building, larger than the one at Richmond, it was managed by a Mr Johnston from Drury Lane, who brought a number of good plays down from London. But either it made a loss, or Mr Paine got tired of his responsibilities as an impresario, because in 1777 he leased it to Joseph Fox, a tavern keeper in Bow Street, Covent Garden.

Fox was an odd character, by all accounts. 'He could combine twenty occupations without being clever in one, a pretty general characteristic of country managers in those days. He was actor, fiddler, painter, tailor, besides sheet faker and bill sticker on occasions.' When showing Sheridan round the theatre, he pointed out with great pride that he had done everything himself.

But he made a good job of it. Freshly decorated and equipped with new machinery, the theatre reopened with *Jane Shore* performed by a company from the Theatre Royal in London, together with a concert given by the famous prima donna, Signorina Storace. A series of well known plays was staged, with London casts that included the Wards, the Farrens, Dighton and Creswick—to say nothing of the celebrated Mrs Baddeley, whose rendering of Fanny in *The Clandestine Marriage* pleased King George III so much that he commissioned Zoffany to paint her portrait in this role. In 1779 a special box was emblazoned with the Ducal arms when the Duke and Duchess of Cumberland came to see *The School for Scandal*, and that same season Mrs Robinson made her Brighton debut in the role of Perdita.

The Prince of Wales, of course, was a keen theatre-goer. (His admiration for leading ladies also extended to Fox's attractive daughter Elizabeth—who became his mistress, and is believed to have borne him a son by the name of George Seymour Crole.) In Brighton the Prince and Mrs Fitzherbert would sometimes visit the theatre as much as three times a week. Under the spur of their patronage, productions were not only up to London standards but often very elaborate. For example, *The Tempest* (not as

Shakespeare wrote it, but as Dryden and Davanent altered it) was staged 'with Music, Machinery, Decorations, and Incidents proper to the Play, with the Representation of a Ship in Distress, and afterwards Wrecked'. Pantomimes, or what we would now call variety shows, were as lavish as anything to be seen in the capital. One of them featured an Irish giant over 8 feet in height, followed by a Harlequin who 'jumped down his own throat' (which sounds like a curious contortion) and concluded with 'Views of the Steine, the Libraries, Orchestra, etc, and a dance by the characters'.

There were also some flops. Amateur theatricals were all the rage at this period, and one production turned out to be so excruciatingly bad that the Prince 'nearly cracked his sides with mirth'. On another occasion Lord Barrymore made a disastrous appearance as Bobadil. It seems that this normally fearless young man, who relished a scrap as much as swapping witticisms in a duchess' drawing room, was unaccountably seized by an outbreak of stage fright. 'Being under the influence of timidity', he confessed. Afterwards he worked off his feelings on Fox's son Joseph. The lad was obliged to put up his fists, and they had a fine old set-to on the Steine, with the Prince acting as referee between the Earl and—let's get it right—the unsuspecting uncle of his son-to-be.

All in all, however, the Brighton theatre made an impressive start. But Fox never got on well with his landlord, and the time came when he decided to invest in a bigger place of his own. Without warning, he closed the old theatre down and built a new one in Duke Street. Constructed mainly of wood, with a plain tiled roof, it was put up in a matter of weeks. Yet the interior was so elegantly fitted out that it was judged to be 'little inferior to the Haymarket'.

The Duke Street Theatre opened on 13 July 1790 with a series of programmes ranging from opera to topical extravaganzas. Audiences were treated to *Don Juan* (with a 'beautiful display of the Fiery Abyss') and a *Tom Thumb* of which the climax was Tom's 'emancipation from his confinement in the abdomen of the Red Cow'. But by far the biggest hits were *The Triumph of Liberty, or The Destruction of the Bastille*, complete with drawbridge and moat, dungeon and tortures (of course, it was very contemporary) and *The Beggars' Opera*, with Mrs Anna Maria Crouch in the lead. This lady was considered to be the best singer of her day. It was said that 'so sweet a countenance, elegant person and ravishing voice were not to be found united in one individual twice in a century'.

Not surprisingly, the Prince was captivated. As a result, her ménage à trois—which comprised Lieutenant Crouch, an impecunious naval officer, and Michael Kelly, the Irish singer who played opposite her—was augmented by the stout shape of the Prince of Wales. This liaison lasted long enough for him to give her a bond of £10,000 and settle £400 a year on her husband to prevent him from bringing an action.

The bond she wisely discounted for a thousand guineas in cash. But soon afterwards she was badly injured in a carriage accident, and retired to Brighton, where she died some years later—still in the devoted arms of Mr Kelly. In the meantime the Prince, switching from mistresses to matrimony and back again, was once more united with Mrs Fitzherbert.

CHAPTER 8
Chinoiserie

The Prince was 'too much every lady's man to be the man of any lady' (as Sheridan used to say) for Mrs Fitzherbert to treat his casual affairs too seriously. Constancy was the last thing she could expect from such an emotional flibberty-gibbet. But Lady Jersey was a different matter. Though nine years older than himself, and already a grandmother, Frances, Countess of Jersey, was still a woman of undeniable attractions. She was not only beautiful and fascinating (wrote Mary Frampton in her Journal), but also clever and unprincipled. And every day it was becoming clearer that the Prince had fallen under her spell.

The trouble was that he wanted both women at once. This, as his wife, Mrs Fitzherbert could not accept. But unfortunately for her, their marriage was not valid in the eyes of the law. It never would be. Which meant that legally, if not morally, he was free to marry again.

If Mrs Fitzherbert saw the malicious hand of her rival behind the brutal letter of dismissal the Prince suddenly sent her in June 1794, she was probably not mistaken. Actually it was his debts which compelled him to get officially married at last. These now exceeded £640,000, and the interest on them alone outran his income. He owed his tailors nearly £35,000; his coachmaker and horse-dealer £40,000; his friends at least as much again. The members of his household had not been paid for months. True, much of the money had been spent rebuilding Carlton House, and in laying the foundations of his splendid collections of pictures, silver and porcelain that have since become part of Britain's national heritage. But these arrears had to be settled.

19. A portrait of Beau Brummell in his heyday by J. Cook (after a miniature). The Prince Regent was his friend and patron for 20 years but they quarrelled in 1813. It was a final irony for one renowned for his exquisite taste and manners that he should die in poverty and madness in a French asylum

Lady Jersey (who could not, of course, marry him herself, already having a husband) saw the chance to increase her own influence by persuading him to sever his connection with Mrs Fitzherbert, while manoeuvring him towards marriage with his cousin, the unattractive Caroline of Brunswick. 'One damned Frau is as good as another' shrugged the Prince, comprehending that he must not so much marry money as contract a suitable state alliance that would end his insolvency.

Caroline he found distasteful from the moment they met. Hardly a word was exchanged between them. Averting his eyes, he called pointedly for a glass of brandy. But since she was his meal-ticket, the marriage had to proceed. Giving vent to his feelings when riding past Mrs Fitzherbert's house, he asked his brother to tell Maria that she was the only woman he would ever love. And as he walked towards the altar he muttered the same thing to his escort. The wedding night itself he spent drunk in the fireplace; while Lady Jersey played her own devious game by putting Epsom salts in the Princess' supper. Having got herself appointed Lady of the Bedchamber to the Princess of Wales, she was always at hand to ensure that nothing went right between husband and wife.

Two months later the Prince took his bride to Brighton. A brilliant round of festivities greeted the Royal couple. There were grand reviews and field days, at which the Prince of Wales' Regiment, renamed the 10th Hussars, appeared in a splendid new uniform designed by their Colonel-in-Chief. They attended the opening service of the new Chapel Royal in Prince's Place, and entertained the Stadtholder, who had just escaped from Holland, leaving his country in the hands of the French. (A soporific monarch, it was his custom to fall asleep at the theatre or at a ball, uttering loud but contented snores.)

In an unpublished memoir an onlooker named Feist recalls: 'Very soon after their marriage, they came down to Brighton together, and the idlers, of whom I was one, had many occasions to see the Princess. She appeared to most persons to be what is commonly called a pretty woman—not a Fitzherbert, certainly—but a woman whom a husband might admire who looked not wholly to beauty, and could be satisfied with the gentle virtues and faithful affections of the sex. But rumours of disagreements soon began to spread. There was a Lady Jersey who was attached to the household of the Princess. This lady had the untoward reputation of fomenting the discords of the newly married couple.'

Which was only too true. If the Princess did her best to appear cheerful in public, behind the scenes Lady Jersey was up to her tricks. She arranged for the poor woman to be given frisky, unmanageable horses to ride at reviews. She mixed spirits in her wine to make her chatter irresponsibly at table. Lady Jersey's mental cruelty, as we would call it, encompassed drinking from the Prince's glass in front of her, and flaunting on her arm a pearl bracelet that the Prince had given to his bride and then taken away again.

But in the end she went too far when she intercepted a packet of letters which the Princess had written home to her mother. In these, Caroline described the British Royal Family—especially 'de old Begum' as she called her mother-in-law—in picturesquely unflattering terms. Exhaustive enquiries were made at the Old Ship Inn and Charing Cross, the two coach terminals. But no trace of the missing letters could be found. Only some months later, when the Queen acidly quoted some of her uncomplimentary remarks, did it become clear where Lady Jersey had taken them, and she was obliged to resign from the Household. (By this time, despite her age, she had become pregnant again. Some months later the *Herald* announced that she had given birth to a son in Brighton, which gave more food for thought to the gossips.)

The Princess was also expecting a baby. Though there were hopes in Brighton that she would remain at the Pavilion for her confinement, she returned to Carlton House where on 17 January 1796 'after a terrible hard labour for about twelve hours' she gave birth to a daughter. Five weeks later the baby was christened Charlotte Augusta in honour of her two grand-mothers. And soon after this the Prince—who felt that his duty was done but was too sensitive to stand scenes—sent his wife a message through his Chamberlain that he intended never to share the same room with her again. He was determined that they should now live apart.

His decision was greeted with opprobrium. Whereupon, denied his father's agreement to a formal separation from a woman he hated, exasper-ated by vulgar attacks by the press (which was inclined to take her side), no longer fascinated by Lady Jersey (who had begun to irritate him), this curiously jumbled man began to plead with Mrs Fitzherbert to resume their old life. All the same it was not until three years later—when both Caroline and Lady Jersey were clearly out of his life, and the Pope had pronounced her free to rejoin her husband 'if he was truly penitent for his sins and sincere in his promise of amendment'—that she consented to do so.

In the meantime he sought refuge with his tailors and bootmakers. It is said that the sculptor Rossi was once made to wait all morning before being admitted to work on a bust of the Prince, because his subject was busy examining patterns presented by two successive tailors, and trying on 40 pairs of boots.

Increasingly, too, he turned for companionship to that elegantly-dressed wit, Beau Brummell. It was while serving in the 10th Hussars that Brummell first met the Prince. He formed part of Caroline's escort when she arrived in England, and was present at their wedding. Shortly after this, while still on duty with them at Brighton, he had the misfortune (or maybe, the good luck?) to fall off his horse during one of the military reviews and break his nose. The horse's hoof turned it up at an impertinent, disdainful angle which precisely suited the role he was to play.

For even the burnished splendour of the Prince of Wales' Regiment, known as 'The Elegant Extracts', failed to meet Brummell's exacting ideals. At Brighton, its officers associated with no one but their own corps. They kept their own blood horses and their own girls. 'At one o'clock they appear on parade to hear the word of command given to the subaltern guard' observed *The Times*, 'afterwards they toss off their goes of brandy, dine about five, and come about eight to the theatre.' But Captain Brummell's tastes were even less military than this. He didn't like horses, and he spent so much time with his Royal Colonel at the Pavilion that he had trouble in recognising his troop when he went on parade.

Before long he left the army and took a house in Chesterfield Street to indulge in his preference for the leisured ease of a young man of fashion. Unlike in France, where women gave the *ton*, it was men who set the pace in

England—and women were more influenced by men's opinions than their own. Being fully aware of this fact, Brummell set out to establish a superiority less of birth and money than of elegance and taste.

Soon he had become the high priest of Dandyism. The Dandy can best be described as a make-believe officer about town, wearing his own special uniform and devoting an exquisite amount of care to its appearance. Perhaps it was having been in the army that gave George Brummell his unchallenged leadership of this coterie. 'To be a Dandy was to belong to an exclusive social set without the risks or responsibilities of naval or military men' suggests the social historian Dr Donald Low. 'The Dandy was detached from the vulgar concerns of the day. He was a bachelor, a leader of fashion, and—in some few instances—a wit.'

Wattier's at the corner of Bolton Street and Piccadilly was the Dandy headquarters. It was named after Prinny's former chef. Here, drinking and gambling for high stakes, would be found elegant sprigs such as Lord Yarmouth (whose mother, the Marchioness of Hertford was shortly to join the band of Prinny's matronly mistresses, while he himself became the model for both Thackeray's Lord Steyne and Disraeli's Lord Monmouth). Or that polished young roué Lord Petersham. Or William Spenser, the society poet, along with a few young officers such as Herbert Taylor, Arthur Upton, James Armstrong and 'Kangaroo' Cooke. Also 'Monk' Lewis, who had a tendency to tears. Once asked why he was crying, Lewis replied: 'Oh, the Duchess spoke so very kindly to me.'

'My dear fellow,' responded his friend Armstrong, 'pray don't cry. I daresay she didn't mean it.'

If much of the wit of that period would hardly raise a chuckle in an American chat show, its humour lay in a droll, laconic delivery that emphasised the absurd and the trivial. Brummell, for instance, on being commiserated for having gout, replied affably: 'Oh, I should not mind so much, but it is in my *favourite* leg.' And when asked if he had ever seen such an unseasonable summer in Brighton, he drawled: 'Yes, last winter.'

Hazlitt called him 'the greatest of small wits'. To an unpopular peer who talked of keeping a coach for his friends, the Beau remarked: 'You should keep a vis-a-vis, and you will always have a vacant place.'

Once, when invited to dine in unfashionable Bloomsbury, he enquired offhandedly whether it was necessary to change post-horses en route. And to a society hostess who asked if he never ate vegetables, he replied, after pause for thought, 'Madam, I once ate a pea.'

Despite his reputation for having an acid tongue, Brummell was endowed with an imperturbable amiability, according to a fellow-dandy and diarist, Tom Raikes. On matters of taste and dress his opinions were implicitly followed. He disapproved of the Macaronis' gaudy ostentation—the striped velvets and satins with spangles, the blue-powdered hair, red-heeled shoes and feathered hats of which the Prince and his friend Fox were so fond—just as he deplored the shabby blue coats and buff waistcoats (representing the American colours) which some Whigs wore to annoy the King.

The sartorial example he set was simple rather than flamboyant. Elegance, he claimed, should be achieved by the cut of the clothes, the immaculate gloss of the boots, the spotless white linen, the fit of the gloves.

He favoured a high stiff collar, and a woollen coat with brass buttons worn buttoned tightly over the waist, its tails tucked into Hessian boots.

But above all he introduced two innovations which revolutionised men's dress for nearly a century. First, the use of starch; so that henceforth the well dressed man's neck was encircled not by a baggy length of often grubby cloth, but by the finest and cleanest muslin standing stiffly under his chin, meticulously tied and systematically creased. ('When he first appeared in this stiffened cravat, its sensation was prodigious' commented the *Spy*, 'Dandies were struck dumb with envy, and washerwomen miscarried.') His second invention was permanently unwrinkled pantaloons. The bottoms of the trousers were held down by buttoned straps which passed under the arch of the foot.

Yet while claiming that the severest mortification a gentleman could incur was to attract notice in the street by his appearance, Brummell encouraged myths about himself. It became known that his boots were cleaned in champagne; that he employed two separate glove-makers (one for thumbs, and the other for the fingers); that in an age when most people avoided soap and water he scrubbed his face with a pig's-bristle brush until he looked 'very much like a man in the scarlet fever'. It was an open secret that he spent hours knotting his cravat so that it should be exactly right. Friends who called would encounter his valet with a dozen or so crumpled pieces of muslin over his arm, which were described as 'our failures'. Often the Prince of Wales would drop by in the morning to watch his toilette and learn the proper technique. Sometimes he sat there so late that he would send away his horses and insist on Brummell giving him a quiet dinner, which (Raikes tells us) usually ended in a 'deep potation'.

Before long the protégé had made a disciple of the Prince. They had the same tailors—Schweitzer & Davidson and Guthrie in Cork Street, Weston & Mayer in Conduit Street. But if the high neck cloths were a clever device to hide the Prince's swollen glands, there was little that could be done to disguise his mounting girth. Now approaching 40, Prinny was becoming Falstaffian enough for Charles Lamb to quip:

By his bulk and by his size
  By his oily qualities

This (or else my eyesight fails)
  This should be the Prince of Whales

Yet once reunited with Mrs Fitzherbert at the Pavilion, the next few years were probably the happiest he ever spent. To be sure, the informality of his youth was giving way to what Lady Jerningham termed 'a proper subordination'; so that life at the Pavilion resolved itself into a routine of small and decorous (though by no means sober) evening parties, occasionally relieved by a touch of hilarity.

Punctually at six the Prince sat down to dinner, and often did not rise from the table until eleven. By this time he was liable to be well in his cups, beating time to the music on the dinner gong. Mrs Creevey told her husband that one evening he began shooting with an air-gun at a target placed at the end of the drawing room. He was apparently quite a good shot;

I think your Comforters are bigger than my Johns.

Won't you take another Comforter? we must make haste, I expect Noodle here presently.

DARBY JOHN

Fishes of Characatures lent out for the Evening

Pub.d Oct.r 21 1802 by S.W. Fores N.o 50 Piccadilly

A BRIGHTON BREAKFAST or *Morning Comforts* *Fashionable Follies. Plate 1.st*

20. This cartoon of 1802 depicts Mrs Fitzherbert awaiting the arrival of the Prince. The artist has capitalised on her ample figure and large nose but for Maria the years between 1802 and 1806 were happy because she and the Prince were reconciled

the trouble started when he made his guests do the same. 'Lady Downshire hit a fiddler in the dining room, Miss Johnstone a door, and Bloomfield the ceiling.'

Two days later she reported that a German Baron was preparing a Phantasmagoria at the Pavilion, and that Mrs Fitzherbert was chuckling at the thought of what he might do to a diffident lady called Miss Johnstone in the dark.

As it turned out, the Baron was far too preoccupied with his apparatus for the Storm and Thunder, Lightning and Rain, or dressing himself up as a Ghastly Phantom of Death, to think about Miss Johnstone. Instead the excitement was provided by Sheridan. Once the lights were extinguished, he slipped over and sat on the lap of a haughty Russian Countess, causing her to yell like a maniac. Another evening—knowing how fond Mrs Fitzherbert was of her whist—the irrepressible playwright came into the drawing room disguised as a Bow Street Runner as the ladies sat over their cards, and proceeded to arrest old Lady Sefton on the pretence that she was playing an illegal game of faro.

In those days, says Raikes, the Prince made the Brighton Races the gayest scene of the year in England.

'The Pavilion was full of guests; the Steyne was crowded with all the rank and fashion from London during that week; the best horses were brought from Newmarket and the North to run at these races, on which enormous sums were depending; and the course was graced by the handsomest equipages. The "legs" and betters, who had arrived in shoals, used to assemble on the Steyne at an early hour to commence their operations on the first day, and the buzz was tremendous, till Lord Foley and Mellish, the two great confederates of that day, would approach the ring; and then a sudden silence ensued, to await the opening of their betting books. They would come on perhaps smiling, but mysterious, without making any demonstration; at last Mr Jerry Cloves would say, "Come, Mr Mellish, will you light the candle, and set us-a-going?" Then, if the Master of Buckle would say, "I'll take three to one about 'Sir Solomon'" the whole pack opened, and the air resounded with every shade of odds and betting. About half an hour before the signal of departure for the hill, the Prince himself would make his appearance in the crowd—I think I can see him now, in a green jacket, a white hat, and tight nankeen pantaloons and shoes, distinguished by his high-bred manner and handsome person: he was generally accompanied by the late Duke of Bedford, Lord Jersey, Charles Wyndham, Shelley, Brummell, M. Day, Churchill, and, oh! extraordinary anomaly! the little old Jew, Travis, who, like a dwarf of old, followed in the train of royalty.

'The Downs were soon covered with every species of conveyance, and the Prince's German waggon and six bay horses [so were barouches called when first introduced at that time]—the coachman on the box being replaced by Sir John Lade—issued out of the gates of the Pavilion, and, gliding up the green ascent, was stationed close to the grand stand, where it remained the centre of attraction for the day. At dinner-time the Pavilion was resplendent with lights, and a sumptious banquet was served to a large party; while those who were not included in that invitation found a dinner with every luxury at the club-house on the Steyne, kept by Raggett, where the cards and dice from St James's Street were not forgotten.'

Raggett's was the Dandies' headquarters in Brighton, and play ran just as high. Moreover, if the men now appeared clad in dark blue or forest-green coats with gilt buttons and white pantaloons, the women had discarded their former rainbow-coloured dresses in favour of clinging gowns of white and grey and the palest pink. Their towering headdresses of waving plumes had given way to simply dressed, unpowdered hair à la Grécque. Yet the Steine presented as debonair a spectacle as ever, and the equipages that 'tooled' each other around were a show in themselves.

Lord Petersham drove a curricle with horses' and servants' liveries all the same shade of brown (which happened to be the name of his current mistress.) Tommy Onslow chose an all-black effect, thereby earning the disapproval of the Four-in-Hand Club. Mr Mellish went in for white, even powdering his face, so that his black hair and moustachios were the only things not chalk-coloured about him. Sir John Lade dressed his postilions in harlequin liveries.

But perhaps the most striking sight on the Steine was an individual named Cope, whom no one seemed to know, though he attracted everyone's attention. He was simply referred to as The Green Man.

'He dressed in green pantaloons, green waistcoat, green frock, green cravat: and though his ears, whiskers, eyebrows and chin were powdered, his countenance, no doubt from the reflection of his clothes, was also green' (says the Annual Register for 1806). 'He ate nothing but greens, fruits and vegetables; had his rooms painted green, and furnished with a green sofa,

21. Sake Deen Mahomed, shampooing surgeon to George IV, in his ceremonial dress of green and gold and scarlet. His life was as colourful as his clothes. He was born at Patna, India, visited Ireland and eloped with a pretty girl, set up his vapour baths at Brighton in 1786 and built up an illustrious clientele. He lived to the ripe old age of 102

green chairs, green tables, green bed and green curtains. His gig, his livery, his portmanteau, his gloves and his whip were all green. With a green silk handkerchief in his hand, and a large watch chain with green seals, fastened to the green buttons of his green waistcoat, he paraded every day on the Steine.' The windows filled with ladies whenever he passed, and one of them expressed her opinion in verse: 'Green garters, green hose, and deny it who can, The brains, too, are green of this green little man.'

Feist remembers how Willis the tailor used to parade the Steine with the fashionable crowd. Looking so elegant that his connection with 'the shop-board' was never suspected, he would bow politely to his customers, who wondered who this dandified figure could be. One gentleman enquired his name.

'Made your breeches, Sir, made your breeches,' replied the bowing Willis. His words were spoken in such a manner that he was understood to say 'Major Bridges'. As such he was accepted among the company until someone asked him what his regiment was.

'Made your breeches, Sir, made your breeches.'

'Yes, but what regiment, if I may be so bold to enquire?' asked a Colonel.

'Made your breeches, Sir, and your coat too. I am Willis the tailor, at your service.'

This was considered to be 'tolerably droll' in the argot of Jane Austen's day, even if social distinctions were no longer quite so clearly marked in the new world of the nineteenth century.

But droller still were the Prince's oriental experiments. Realising, after his reconciliation with Mrs Fitzherbert that the Pavilion was too small for his needs, he embarked on some startling architectural adventures that were to culminate in the most remarkable Indo-Chinese palace ever to take root on English soil.

Its development was piecemeal. An observer from the drawing room of the Old Ship in 1801 would have been as incredulous to see Prinny's pleasure dome 16 years later as the visitor today may be to learn that most of the Prince's life in Brighton—certainly the roistering and high jinks—took place in quite a conventional villa and not the poem to autocracy that now greets one's eyes.

As a first step to enlarge the building two small wings were added, containing a dining room and an additional drawing room. But at this point the Prince was presented with several pieces of very beautiful Chinese wallpaper, which he had put up in the gallery. Next he had the rest of the interior redecorated to conform with the gallery.

This was not so much of an innovation as it might seem: the vogue for chinoiserie had been considered chic for some time. It was more of a revival of the earlier *goût chinois*. Lady Bessborough wrote in 1805: 'Today I have been going all over the Pavilion, which is really beautiful in its way. I did not think the strange Chinese shapes and columns could have looked so well. It is like Concetti in poetry, in outré and false taste, but for the kind of thing is as perfect as it can be, and the Prince says he had it so because at the time there was such a cry against the French things, etc, that he was afraid of his furniture being accus'd of Jacobinism.'

Concurrently the Prince commissioned William Porden, who was building Steine House for Mrs Fitzherbert, to design some great new stables.

These, however, were to be constructed in the Mughal style—possibly to commemorate the extension of the British Empire in India.

The Stables with their Hindu exterior and immense glass dome—acknowledged as one of the wonders of Europe—were completed in 1805 on what had once been the Promenade Grove. East Street now bisected the Prince's property and ran almost under the windows of his house. So he arranged with the Town Commissioners to replace it by a thoroughfare along the boundary, which became known as New Road. And since up to this moment he had only rented the Pavilion from Weltje, the Prince of Wales extricated himself from the anomalous position of being his own cook's tenant by purchasing the house for £17,300. (Having bought the original property from Thomas Kemp in 1786 for £3,000, Weltje should have run laughing all the way to the bank. Instead he suddenly expired at the tea-table from a surfeit, it might be surmised, of his own delicious gingerbread.)

The Prince's grounds now formed a small enclosed park of about eight acres. But beyond having them landscaped by Humphry Repton, and collecting quantities of Chinoiserie, the Prince made no further alterations to the Pavilion for another 12 or 13 years. Yet as he gazed at the soaring pinnacles of the Royal Stables and the lotus-shaped glass leaves of their huge dome shining in the sun, he must have felt that this palatial accommodation for his horses contrasted oddly with the chaste classical elevations of his own relatively modest abode. We know that he dreamed of the regal splendour of the Mughal courts, and that nothing would have pleased him better than to own an Indian palace. Indeed Repton was commissioned to supply drawings in 1806.

The truth is that another avalanche of debts—the Stables alone cost £55,000—prevented the Prince's romantic visions from taking shape. It was the old problem, money. So for the time being the plans had to be shelved.

In the quarter of a century since he first came to Brighton, the world had been manufacturing history at a remarkable rate. France had galloped from autocracy to dictatorship with scarcely a pause for democracy on the way. The Americans had confirmed their independence. Clarkson and Wilberforce had begun their campaign for the abolition of the slave trade; Warren Hastings had been impeached for consolidating the sub-continent that was to be the core of Britain's next empire. Frederick of Prussia and Catherine the Great had died. The King of France had been beheaded, the King of England had lost his wits.

Hovering impatiently on the threshold of power, the Prince began to cold shoulder Mrs Fitzherbert again; partly because he was afraid that the association with a 'Papist' might damage his chances of becoming Regent, but chiefly because he had fallen in love with the stately, puritanical Marchioness of Hertford—whom the Hon. Mrs Calvert cattily described as 'without exception the most forbidding, haughty, unpleasant looking woman I ever saw'.

The ultimate break with poor Maria occurred when he refused her a place at his table for the grand fete held to celebrate the inauguration of his Regency. Ever since their secret marriage he had promised that he would formally recognise her position in society as soon as it was within his means to do so. But that was before Lady Hertford had usurped her seat in his affections.

'You know, Madam, you have no place,' he now told her.

'None, Sir, but such as you desire to give me.'

They never spoke to each other again.

As Regent, he found his responsibilities daunting. Above all, there was the worrying question of whether to dismiss the Tory government and call in the Whigs. There were also the dispatch boxes. 'Playing at King is no sinecure' he complained wearily to Lord Dundas after dealing with a mountain of papers. At the first possible moment he escaped to Brighton, where politics were not discussed. No members of the government were invited to the Pavilion, and he could indulge in the pleasant prospect of fulfilling his architectural dreams.

The purchase of Marlborough House on the north side of the Pavilion gave the necessary space to expand the Pavilion into a palace. Instead of commissioning Repton, whose early designs had a distinctly Chinese flavour, he employed John Nash as architect. First, however, he asked Wyatt, the Surveyor-General of the Office of Works to provide an estimate for the conversion. If he intended him to carry out the task himself, this became impossible when Wyatt was killed in a carriage accident in 1813. (But for which, suggests Antony Dale, we might have had a Gothic Palace at Brighton.)

Nash, who was already engaged on the grandiose project which resulted in the creation of Regent Street, Carlton House Terrace and Buckingham Palace, began work on the Pavilion in 1815. Marlborough House was demolished, and the present Music Room built on its site. To balance the proportions, a Banqueting Room replaced the oblique wings added earlier by Holland.

'They had their tent-shaped spires and their oriental façade of today, without the trellised verandahs' notes Dale. 'Between them Holland's Pavilion remained intact, and its simple bowed façade provided a most incongruous appearance with the new Oriental box-like wings. However during 1818 the remainder of the east front was brought into harmony with the wings and the verandahs added. The north and west fronts followed in 1819, so that by 1820 the exterior of the Pavilion had assumed the form in which we see it today. At the same time the underground passage was built connecting the Pavilion with the stables. The only remaining addition was the conversion of the Ballroom of the Castle Hotel to the south-east into the Royal Chapel in 1821.'

Meanwhile the interior of the Pavilion was being redecorated in the exuberant Chinese style that still meets our eyes, which among other things included delicate bamboo balustrades and exotic palm tree supports—all made of cast-iron and copper.

An Indian building with a Chinese décor! Most people were horrified. 'The Pavilion was a masterpiece of bad taste' wrote the Comtesse de Boigne, who as little Adèle had admired the Prince's shoe buckles some 30 years previously. 'Here at immense expense had been brought together from the four corners of the globe a collection of curiosities—of the most sumptuous kind, admittedly—all heaped together under the eight (or is it ten?) cupolas of this bizarre, ugly palace, this hotch-potch of styles completely

THE PAVILION, BRIGHTON.

22. A view showing the west front of the Royal Pavilion which appears to be positively bristling with minarets. The sketch shows the porte-cochère in use. Today, visitors still enter the Pavilion through this gateway

23. The east front of the Royal Pavilion. To the right is St Peter's Church designed by Charles Barry and consecrated in 1828. A statue of George IV stands in front of the Pavilion and the cost of erecting it in 1828 was met by public subscription. The statue can still be seen today but on a site to the north of the Pavilion

lacking in unity, and surely not worthy of the name of architecture. The arrangement of the interior was no better, and certainly had nothing to do with art.

'But there' she conceded, 'my criticism ends. In no other establishment was there a better understanding of the arts of comfort and pleasure; and having—as a salaam to the canons of good taste—disparaged this fantastic

24. *A visitor to the Royal Pavilion in 1818 wrote 'The kitchens and larders are admirable—such contrivances for roasting, boiling, baking, stewing, frying, steaming and heating'. The kitchen was also adjacent to the dining room which meant guests enjoyed the luxury of hot food. So often in great houses of that period, kitchens were far removed from the dining rooms, with the danger that food was frequently spoiled or cold by the time it reached the table*

amalgam of curiosities, one could enjoy oneself endlessly in examining all the fine detail of this costly extravaganza.'

Perhaps it was Sydney Smith who most succinctly summed up public opinion of the day when, on catching sight of the building, he turned to his companion and remarked: 'One would think that St Paul's Cathedral had come to Brighton, and pupped.'

Indeed it was not until Sir Osbert Sitwell extolled its virtues 50 years ago that modern taste, conditioned by international travel, began to appreciate the depth of romantic inspiration and breath-taking loveliness that makes the Pavilion unique.

Of all Prinny's legacies, it is the most personal. Yet it brought him little pleasure. For a few months in 1816 some of the former sparkle was revived when Princess Charlotte, lively and excited by her engagement to the young Prince Leopold of Saxe-Coburg-Saalfeld, revelled in the exotic Chinese surroundings and infected everyone with her happiness. Though her father was confined to a wheelchair with gout, he joined in the gaiety, and even arranged for a complicated apparatus to be made to lift him on to his horse. The wedding took place on 2 May 1816. But soon after the nation had been delighted by the news that Charlotte was expecting a child, came the shock of the death of both mother and baby in childbirth.

In January 1820, while lying ill with a heavy cold in Brighton, the

13. Royal Pavilion under snow

14. Pavilion Gardens in Spring

Regent learnt that his father was dying. After spending most of the spring convalescing at the Pavilion—during which he studied all the prayer books in the library hoping to find a precedent that would support his determination to exclude his wife's title and name from the liturgy—George IV was finally crowned King at Westminster on 19 July the following year. His coronation banquet, the last and most lavish ever to be given in England, was marred only by the unseemly incident in which Princess Caroline, who regarded herself rightfully to be Queen, was turned away at the door.

At the Old Ship, plans for the Coronation celebrations in Brighton were discussed by the magistrates. As usual there was to be 'the roasting of three oxen whole, for distribution among the populace, with a suitable quantity of bread and strong beer; bonfires and a grand display of fireworks; and a variety of sports and diversions to give a merry complexion to the day'. A clergyman protested at the barbarous custom of roasting oxen, but Mr Myrtle the butcher won general approval by declaring that the carcase of a fine fat bullock was a 'noble and gratifying object'. His view was borne out on the day itself when the *Brighton Herald* reported that 'even the most delicate and beautiful females of fashion suffered themselves to be squeezed most indelicately in the throng of people waiting to be served'.

But while rockets hissed past coloured balloons, and the population was enjoying itself—including the excisemen, who were determined to demonstrate their loyalty—certain other people had a field day in the deserted stableyard of the Old Ship. At a given signal, a band of smugglers emerged from their hiding place on the beach with about 30 kegs of Dutch gin, which they slung on the backs of their horses and vanished as furtively as they had come, before anyone could realise what was happening.

Angry though the authorities may have felt to be caught off their guard, the rest of the people were in excellent humour, and the King could feel satisfied that he had received, as Sir Walter Scott put it, 'a general welcome from his subjects'.

'He is at length King. Will his resentments still attach to his crown?' wrote poor balding Brummell who, having fallen foul of Prinny, was now penniless in Calais. But when George IV passed through that port a little later, he made a point of avoiding his old friend, though a single kind gesture would have saved him from a miserable end. Nor did he display any grief when the news came that Princess Caroline had died, apparently from the shock of being denied her place at the Coronation. Quite to the contrary. 'This is the happiest day of my life!' the King is said to have exclaimed.

After 15 years as his closest confidante, Lady Hertford had also been discarded. He was now under the dominance of Lady Conyngham, a fat, kindly, rich and rapacious woman on whom he clearly doted. Installed in the end house at Marlborough Row, this lady of ample proportions, who had been part of the fashionable Brighton scene for at least 20 years, became the undisputed mistress of the Pavilion, and apparently of the King as well. 'What an atmosphere the King lives in!' commented Lady Anne Becket. 'He never, since he has been at Brighton, has left his own room, except to walk across at half past three or four to Lady C's house, and at six to walk back again; he then dresses and comes to dinner, and that is the whole of his air and exercise.'

25. The fashionable scene at Brighton set against a multitude of domes and minarets. Beauties of Brighton *drawn by A. Crowquill etched by G. Cruikshank*

Yet now that the Pavilion was finally completed, the King seemed to have lost his delight in it. Swelling with dropsy, and morbidly sensitive about his appearance, he hated the idea of being spied on by the Brighton crowds (who so much annoyed Queen Victoria later on). More and more he forsook the place on which he had centred his enthusiasm for over 40 years, to live in dreary seclusion at Windsor.

He spent much of the day in bed, having novels read to him by the pretty actress, Eliza Chester (Scott and Jane Austen were still his favourite authors). Occasionally he would drive out in a little pony chaise to see his pet giraffe in the menagerie, where he would sit sipping cherry brandy with a cockatoo sitting on his arm. Greville tells us that he took a perverse pleasure in astounding his ministers—Wellington included—by pretending that he had fought at Waterloo, and led a dashing charge of dragoons at the Battle of Salamanca, disguised at General Bock.

'He was indeed the most extraordinary compound of talent, wit, buffoonery, obstinacy and good feeling—in short a medley of the most opposite qualities with a preponderance of good that I ever saw in any character in my life,' was the Duke of Wellington's summing up of the man who had done more than any other to put Brighton on the map.

During the King's last visit in 1828 a Privy Council was held at the Pavilion, with Catholic Emancipation on the agenda. In anticipation of which four carriages from London, each containing a pianoforte, were seen to unload their contents in the premises. Food for thought to musicologists! But rather than dwell on those final years of his life, when the King was clearly failing in mind and body, let us take our leave of Prinny at Christmas in 1823.

There he is in the Music Room receiving Rossini during the Italian's first visit to England. ('A fat, sallow squab of a man,' is Lady Granville's opinion of the guest, 'but those large languishing eyes and *des traits* justify his thinking himself, as they say he does, something very irresistible.') Yet as the band plays the overture to *La Gazza Ladra* and a selection from *Il Barbiere*, and the composer sings 'Largo al factotum' the King listens entranced. Nor does he show any sign of displeasure when at the end of the performance, as the Coronation March is played, Rossini, uninvited, plumps himself down on a seat by his side. Of all monarchs, he was the first to pay tribute to a maestro.

CHAPTER 9

Georgian Brighton

Regency Brighton! Yes, the term has a pleasantly raffish ring. It stands for a poised sort of elegance, a Byronic brio. It conjures up images of stage-coaches, the Pavilion, crescents of white bow-windowed houses, a graceful style of furniture. It is typified, if you like, by the Old Ship itself—where Byron is believed to have stayed.

Byron's romantic aura (the cricket at Lord's, and the dreaming on tombstones; the rumours of buffoonery in monkish garb, the human skulls filled with burgundy at Newstead Abbey) caught Prinny's eye when the young poet was a guest at the Pavilion in 1808. Then up at Cambridge, Byron spent much of the summer vacation in Brighton. With him were 'Gentleman Jack', the champion boxer; an atractive young girl dressed up as a boy (whom he called his 'brother'); along with a couple of quarrelsome bulldogs and a bear.

His *Juvenile Poems* had just been published, if hardly to critical acclaim. So it is tempting to speculate whether the satire on his critics ('With just enough of learning to misquote') that appeared in *English Bards and Scotch Reviewers* was written at the Old Ship that summer. Probably not. All the evidence suggests that Byron did indeed stay at the Old Ship for a while. But perhaps his bear was too much for Shuckhard and Hicks, for he soon moved to a house in Marine Parade, where apart from sparring with his 'Dear Jack', he spent the time swimming and boating or riding on the Downs. And playing hazard until four in the morning.

In Byron's day—indeed through most of the Regency—the graceful

26. Nicolo Paganini was a brilliant musician but with his lean frame and pale face, his bushy hair and dark clothes, he was a gift to the caricaturists. This representation is one of the more restrained. He attracted crowds wherever he gave concerts and when he performed in the Ballroom of the Old Ship in December 1831, people had to pay 10/- for the privilege of listening to him. The local press were not overawed by his reputation and grumbled because he played his own works exclusively

squares and crescents that are loosely termed 'Regency' were not yet built. Brighton still combined the gaiety and elegance of a town with the charm and prettiness of a country village. Though it is usually regarded as a Regency town, few buildings from that period still survive.

Parts of the Old Ship do, of course, though its structure is much older and the façade has been modernised. Yet the hotel reached its peak during those Regency years, and a whiff of the old atmosphere lingers on as you take tea in the drawing room or dine in the Assembly Rooms. 'Long after the closing of the Castle Hotel the brilliant tradition of the great balls was continued at the Old Ship Hotel' writes Musgrave. 'They were organised by a committee of lady patronesses, with Mrs Fitzherbert at their head. As at Almack's in London, these ladies wielded despotic power in granting admission to what Captain Gronow described as "the seventh heaven of the fashionable world".'

Prince Puckler-Muscau was amused at the trouble people took to get tickets. 'It is an immense favour to obtain one, and for people who do not belong to the very highest or most modish world, very difficult,' he observed in his *Letters on England*. 'Intrigues are set on foot months beforehand, and the lady patronesses flattered in the meanest and most servile manner.' Finding himself 'executed', as he quaintly puts it, to attend one of these grand affairs at the Old Ship, he pronounced that 'In Brighton we find a copy of London in little'.

Once the popularity of great formal balls declined, the renown of the Old Ship was upheld by concerts. 'Most of the concerts of any pretensions which take place in this town are held at the Old Ship Assembly Rooms' states the *Brighton Herald* in 1831. And of these the most notable was a performance given by Niccolo Paganini in December that year. George Augustus Sala, the journalist and war correspondent, tells us that 260 people turned up to hear him play, and paid ten shillings each for the privilege. As so often happens, they had to sit through a dull supporting programme before the maestro made his entrance on to the ballroom balcony. To the newspaper's regret, he played exclusively his own compositions. But this enabled him to introduce his own style, and gave scope to his exquisite skill in executing passages 'such as no other man would ever think of writing'.

'A lean wan gentleman in black with bushy hair' is how George Sala remembers the great violinist. Sala's widowed mother had organised the concert, and when it was time to settle up with Paganini she took young George along with her, thinking perhaps that the sight of a widow with a small child in tow might prevent him from driving too hard a bargain.

Says Sala: 'Mother put down fifty guineas on the table. When I say that he washed his hands in the gold—that he scrabbled at it, as David of old did at the gate—and grasped it and built it up into little heaps, panting the while, I am not in any way exaggerating. He bundled it at last in a blue cotton hankerchief with white spots, and darted from the room. And we—my poor mother convulsively clasping my hand—went out on the landing and were descending the stairs when the mighty violinist bolted again from his bedroom door. "Take that little boy" he said, "take that", and he thrust a piece of paper rolled up almost into a ball into my hand. It was a banknote for fifty pounds.'

The Old Ship's pre-eminence had remained unquestiond until now. But

the expansion of Brighton in the 1820s caused competitors to appear. Dr Hall, who owned the old manor house and a row of buildings known as Steine Place, converted his property into a hotel which he named the Royal York. Even this was not enough to accommodate the crowds of visitors. So in 1826 another splendid pile, the Royal Albion, sprang up on the site of Dr Russell's old house overlooking the sea. It was designed by Wilds and Busby, who that same year rebuilt the Royal Pavilion Hotel in Castle Square.

Moreover, once fashionable attention had begun to turn westwards, the Bedford Hotel was erected in 1829. Here the architect was Thomas Cooper, who constructed some of the houses in Brunswick Square, and also designed the Brighton Town Hall. It was the town's most distinguished hotel, says Dale. 'After the closing of the Pavilion in 1845 all the members of the English Royal family who continued to visit Brighton invariably stayed at the Bedford. Foreign royalties, princes and celebrities on their visits also made it their headquarters.' None the less, the Old Ship continued to attract its traditional clientele, and its Assembly Rooms remained the chief social venue in the town.

But this is running ahead of our story. What we call 'Regency' Brighton was mainly the achievement of three men—Amon Wilds, his son Amon Henry Wilds, and Charles Augustus Busby. Between them the trio did as much for Brighton as the Woods did for Bath, or Nash accomplished in London. They built four, possibly five squares, four crescents, nine terraces, six streets, five churches, as well as a large number of private houses, and other buildings too. It was they who created Brighton's distinctive style

27. A panoramic view of Brighton drawn by John Bruce from the top of St Peter's Church. Behind the Royal Stables (now the Dome) rises the bulk of the new Town Hall designed by Thomas Cooper and erected in 1830. The Steine is not yet embellished with its fountain. It is easy to see how crowded Brighton had become and to understand how Queen Victoria resented the lack of privacy

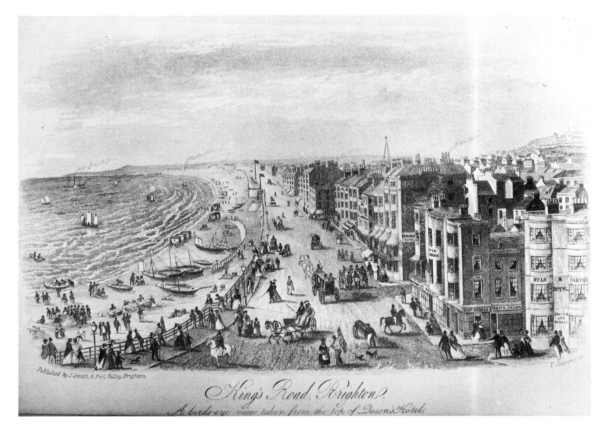

28. A bird's eye of the King's Road, Brighton. The Old Ship is almost opposite the group of three bathing machines

that we know and love. Their work, says Antony Dale, 'was the execution in bricks and stucco of the change wrought by George IV in the less substantial world of taste and fashion'.

The Wilds, père et fils, were building contractors from Lewes whose activities at Brighton began with a chapel in Ship Street erected for Thomas Read Kemp. In 1818 they became involved in the development of Regency Square on what was known as Belle Vue field. They also indulged in a little speculative building of their own in Richmond Terrace and Waterloo Place. But success really came when they teamed up with Charles Busby.

The son of a noted musicologist, Busby studied at the Royal Academy's school of drawing, where he exhibited a 'Design for a Mansion' when he was only 13. Six years later he published a book in which he criticised the Adam brothers' style, and extolled the virtues of Greek architecture. After spending several years in the United States (where his interests ranged from paddle steamers to prisons) he returned to England in 1821 and went into business with Amon Wilds.

Busby and Wilds' first important project was to design the great new estate that Kemp planned to build to the east of the town. Modelled on Regent's Park in London, it was conceived to provide a complex of palatial dwellings that would attract the fashionable world away from the cramped town centre to the spacious seclusion of the clifftop near the race-course. The full splendour of the original concept can only be judged from the architects' drawings, for only half of the houses planned were actually built.

And initially just the façades were constructed, like a stage set—with columned fronts and pagoda-like canopies to the balconies, but simply a shell behind—so that prospective owners could complete the interiors of the buildings to their individual tastes.

At first the estate turned out to be a white elephant. Perhaps it was too far away. Granted, the sixth Duke of Devonshire purchased the shells of No 14 Chichester and No 1 Lewes Crescent, which were adjoining; while the fifth Earl of Bristol (whose father gave his name to so many hotels all over Europe) bought 19 and 20 Sussex Square. But after ten years only 36 of the 105 houses were occupied, and some remained with their carcasses in scaffolding until Thomas Cubitt completed the project in the 1850s. Even so, four prime ministers stayed in Kemp Town. The Earl of Aberdeen took a house in Chichester Terrace for two months during the winter of 1836; Lord John Russell rented 14 Sussex Square for three months in 1838; Sir Robert Peel stayed at 13 Lewes Crescent in 1842 during the Easter Parliamentary recess, and in 1844 Gladstone visited his brother who had leased 5 Sussex Square.

As one of the Lords of the Manor, Thomas Read Kemp ranked second only to Lord Egremont as Brighton's leading citizen. For many years he sat as MP for Lewes. By his marriage to the daughter of Sir Francis Baring, Chairman of the East India Company and founder of the famous banking firm, he inherited a considerable fortune. Yet even for such substantial means the Kemp Town scheme proved too much. In 1837 financial difficulties forced him to withdraw from public life and move to France; sad to say, a proclamation of outlawry against him was nailed to the door of St Peter's Church just before his death in 1844.

Wilds and Busby's next commission was more fortunate. This was the construction of a similar estate on an expanse of waste land to the west of the town and technically in the parish of Hove—which was then still a tiny village clustered around its ruined church and manor house. Work began on what was to be known as Brunswick Town in 1824. First the Terrace was built, and then the Square. Lansdowne Place followed in 1827.

The landowner was the Rev. Thomas Scutt. But Busby seems to have controlled the development of this estate, personally approving the plans submitted by individual builders. Interestingly enough, Antony Dale has unearthed a copy of the specifications for one of the upper houses on the east side of Brunswick Square. This shows both the elevation and ground plan and gives detailed measurements of the internal layout of each floor, including the cellars beneath the road and the stables behind. It is dated 5 July 1827, and stipulates that the complete price of the house 'papered, painted, with all Drains, Shores, and Pavement' was to be £3,000—a not inconsiderable sum, and the equivalent of perhaps £150,000 today.

From the beginning, Brunswick Square was destined for residential homes, in contrast to the Terrace facing the sea, which comprised furnished dwellings that were let on a weekly basis—thus enabling the owners to gain an extra month's rent each year. (So high were Brighton rents, complained a French visitor, that the charge for a single week was as much as a house would cost for a whole year in France.)

Visitors flocked in just the same. In 1828 Sir Robert Peel took 24 Brunswick Terrace for three months, and the Duke of Wellington's elder

29. Originally J.M.W. Turner painted a water-colour of the Chain Pier entitled View of Brighton from the Sea *but, as can be seen from the illustration, it was turned into a very successful engraving which first appeared in 1825. This engraving lends weight to the storminess of the sea and indicates the sort of stress the old pier had to withstand*

brother, the Marquess of Wellesley, spent a month at No 19. Over the next few years there was a stream of famous names, which included the Duke of Gloucester, Lord Brougham (to whom Cannes traces its renown), Gladstone, Lady Palmerston, Prince Metternich and a host of foreign ambassadors.

For a glimpse of the daily life these people led, let us turn to the Comte de la Garde, a French man of letters who visited Brighton in 1827. After a rough crossing from Dieppe, he was clearly enchanted with his first sight of the place as the paddle steamer berthed at the Chain Pier: 'a kind of bridge suspended on chains—a model of grace combined with solidity that was a worthy introduction to the magnificent amphitheatre behind it.'

From here (thriftily avoiding the Royal Albion and the Old Ship, we must assume) he made his way to the Gloucester Hotel in Gloucester Place, to be greeted by 'a polite hostess, attentive servants and—a much greater rarity in Brighton—moderate prices'.

He found the food delicious and his bedroom unexpectedly comfortable. 'An admirable dinner was set before me, consisting of the excellent fish which abound in Brighton; mutton said to be the best in all England—because the Downs which the flocks feed on are impregnated with salt; tasty vegetables even though they had been boiled, and a variety of puddings.' After dinner he was presented with a bootjack and slippers by the valet, who then escorted him up a narrow but well carpeted staircase to his room. He was astonished by the bed. With its four carved pillars of massive mahogany supporting an elegantly draped tester, it was big enough to accommodate at least three people, and the piled mattresses were topped by a thick feather

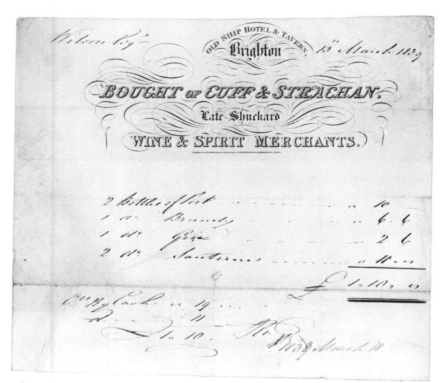

30. An early bill—Cuff and Strachan of the Old Ship—13 March 1839

eiderdown. 'When I had scaled this peaceful fortress (with the aid of a small step ladder) and drawn its double curtains of white muslin, I found myself installed in something like an inner room, as least as spacious as a monk's cell. In safe haven and in lively anticipation of the novel scenes I was about to witness, I had no trouble in sinking into a deep sleep and putting behind me all the fatigues and nausea of the horrible sea-crossing.'

Next morning he was able to take a more careful stock of the room. Its studied neatness, he thought, was a delight to the eye. 'A marble fireplace, extending only a short way into the room, was decorated with a number of graceful little trinkets. The fire-irons had such a polish that they were obviously cleaned every day. The iron grate, a foot high, was filled with coal as black and shining as jet. As to the furnishing, there was a toilet table set out with everything necessary for one's morning ablutions, such as porcelain and Wedgwood basins of various sizes for a variety of purposes; crystal bottles, face and hand towels in linen and cotton, and perfumed Windsor soap. And all this in the bedroom of an inn!'

Obviously no cost accountancy there, nor any fear of guests making off with the contents. One wonders whether La Garde would have been so lyrical about a modern five star hotel, for all its tiled bathrooms and TV sets. He was also impressed by the way that a trim maidservant knocked politely on the door to bring him hot water soon after he woke up (rather than bursting unceremoniously in, as they did on the continent) and took his order for breakfast.

It would be pleasant, of course, to come across so detailed a description from a guest at the Old Ship, where the service and accommodation must have been similar if not better (and more expensive). But La Garde did go to a ball at the Old Ship. 'I was dazzled at my entry by the profusion of lights, the richness of the costumes and the brilliancy of the decorations' says this cosmopolitan *homme du monde*, a relative of the Prince de Ligne who made the famous remark about 'Congress dancing' at the Congress of Vienna (indeed, it was to La Garde that he made it). 'The ladies were dressed in the height of fashion and plentifully adorned with diamonds and other precious stones. They may have lacked something of that piquant *chic* which one finds to perfection only in the Parisienne, but in compensation there was such a freshness of colouring, such a caste of feature and virginal expression that they might have stepped from some delicious canvas of Rafael or Correggio.' The dancers were performing a Scottish reel, which La Garde thought most graceful. Their agility astonished him. He found it curious that the traditionally phlegmatic British should fancy a dance that was a good deal brisker and more sprightly than any Neapolitan tarantella.

Foreign eyes often pick up details that the native observer takes for granted. Strolling along the seafront he admired the width of the streets; the granite pavements on both sides of the road which made walking so agreeable; the elegance of even quite unpretentious houses with their vivid green lawns and little gardens full of flowers. He liked that characteristic Brighton feature, the 'verandah'; each with its own iron trellis work in various designs that projected like a balcony and was topped by a zinc 'tent' striped in various colours. Most of them were covered by rambler-roses or other climbing plants, which gave them some of the indolent gaiety of the Indies. 'Everything about these dwellings' he thought, 'seems designed for people who will go on enjoying them, undisturbed, for ever. Yet in fact their occupants are the merest birds-of-passage!'

Best of all he liked the succession of squares built round lawns, or gardens of flowers and shrubs. They were a pleasant alternative to what would otherwise be a monotonous march of buildings. Each of the gardens was enclosed by an iron fence and only local residents had the key of the gate. As a Parisian, he had to admit that only the old Place-Royale could match the charm of a Brighton crescent.

Wandering into several houses that were still in course of construction, he noticed how, whether large or small, all followed the same basic plan. Only the scale was different. There was no *porte-cochère*. Quite a small doorway led into the hall, from which one entered a parlour that also did duty as a dining room. A narrow staircase led to the first floor which contained two drawing rooms, one large and one small. The bedrooms were on the second floor. The servants slept in the attics and the kitchen was in the basement.

There was a similar uniformity outside. No single house had more than three sash windows in the front. But by joining several houses together, it had been possible to decorate them richly with architectural features borrowed from Greece, Rome or Asia, and thereby produce 'palaces' that were astonishing to a stranger. The use of stucco enabled bricks to be fashioned into pillars and capitals and pediments before being coated with cement and adorned with the most delicate kind of ornament—which, carefully whitened, could easily be taken for Florentine marble.

All this told one at a glance that Brighton was a resort entirely dedicated to the world of fashion. The proximity of London, for one could speak of proximity when public coaches covered the distance in five hours, made Brighton an elegant epitome of the metropolis. 'It has the same luxury, the same glitter' he believed, 'but without that rush of business which in London seems to allow neither place nor time for private pleasures. There are shops in rich variety. Those selling fruit, fish and meat are remarkable for an exquisite cleanliness which one could well wish to see copied elsewhere. The shopkeepers seem to be at pains to avoid offending any of the other senses in an environment where the palate should be one's sole counsellor.'

A paradise lost? Well, perhaps not entirely. In the context of the modern egalitarian world, one could say something of the same sort today (albeit with some reservations). Yet a century and a half ago this cultivated Frenchman also had a few qualifications to his encomiums when invited to dine by Kemp.

His host had only moved into Kemp Town the previous month, and La Garde found 'this newest town in Europe', as he described it, 'as deserted at its birth as Pompei two thousand years after its destruction.'

However on arriving at Kemp's house, he was greeted by a number of retainers in rich liveries who ran out to open the carriage door. Inside, another collection of footmen filled the hall. 'My name, which I gave at the door, was announced four times before I reached the drawing room! According to the English code of manners, I was introduced to each of the guests, whose names were recited to me. Without this piece of protocol, any conversation with them would have been unthinkable, even if one had met them a dozen times before.'

The drawing room was magnificently furnished and sumptuously carpeted. A large crystal chandelier hung in the centre, and the walls were covered with old masters. There were tables full of ornamental tortoiseshell, ivory, gold and silver objets d'art. When the company went downstairs to dine, La Garde was struck by the silver dinner service, and plate engraved with the arms of the Kemp family, that was piled high on the mahogany sideboard.

Prepared by a French chef, the dinner was excellent. But he was astonished how some of the more diehard guests spurned the exquisitely cooked dishes in favour of roast beef or boiled fish, which they proceeded to smother with bottled spices and dressings. He thought it odd that when such expert cooks had been employed at great expense, one should choose to make one's own sauces, and at the table too. Also that custom required the host to carve the poultry and joints, when so many servants were available to do the chore. Another oddity was that champagne was served throughout the meal until replaced by claret with the dessert. In La Garde's opinion it should have been the other way around.

After the ladies had left, the cloth was removed to reveal a magnificent table, around which rare wines (rather than port, as one might have expected) were circulated in crystal decanters mounted on little silver carriages. At the same time, a chamber pot was produced from the sideboard.

'I will say no more than one word about the usage which permits all the gentlemen to retire, one after the other, to a corner of the room—an old fashioned procedure that rather conflicts with the delicacy of modern

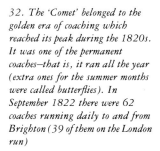

31. The Devil's Dyke has long been a favourite place for excursions and this scene dates from 1827. The Dyke has much to offer—a superb view over the Weald; an intriguing legend about the Devil trying to breach the Downs and flood Sussex; and associations with royalty (King William IV, Queen Adelaide, Queen Victoria and the Prince Consort all made their way to the Dyke). In 1887 a railway was constructed to the Dyke from Aldrington which meant that you could travel direct from Brighton. It was closed in 1939. Due to the foresight of Sir Herbert Carden, the Dyke was purchased on behalf of Brighton so that the beauty spot could be preserved

32. The 'Comet' belonged to the golden era of coaching which reached its peak during the 1820s. It was one of the permanent coaches—that is, it ran all the year (extra ones for the summer months were called butterflies). In September 1822 there were 62 coaches running daily to and from Brighton (39 of them on the London run)

manners' comments La Garde. 'What appears to me even stranger is their invariable habit of drinking the health of the guest who is momentarily away from the table. As what he is doing does not prevent his hearing what is said, he is able to prepare a short speech of reply, which he delivers with due gravity before resuming his place at the table.'

Once coffee was announced, the gentlemen went up to the drawing room, where the chandelier had been lit, and its crystal sparkled in the candlelight. Miss Kemp played the harp and sang airs by Rossini. Some of the guests danced quadrilles and waltzes; a professional musician strummed on the guitar. Finally a sumptuous collation was served before the party broke up.

Another surprise was the way people thought nothing of plunging naked into the sea, even in the depth of winter.

'A hut on wheels was provided with everything that was needed after and during the bathe, such as towels, flannels, and so on. The bather got in. The attendant climbed on to a kind of seat and drove the hut down to the beach until it was in a sufficient depth of water. Then he turned the horse round to face up the beach again, thus enabling the bather to enter the sea very conveniently by a little ladder at the back of the hut. If a lady or a child required just a simple dip, two females seized them by the arms as they emerged from the hut and plunged them into the water three times. The English ascribe considerable virtue to the electric shock administered to the limbs by this sudden immersion in cold salt water.'

If the trip on a cross-channel steampacket had been unpleasant, La Garde's journey on the stage-coach to London was a delightful experience. It took seven hours on a road that was as smooth and well gravelled as a garden path.

'The horses, their harness, and the vehicle itself were of such elegance that a Margrave of Bayreuth or Anspach might well have coveted the whole turn-out for state occasions. To complete the illusion, a fanfare on the posthorn was performed with considerable panache by the guard sitting at the back of the coach. His instrument, far more harmonious than the little trumpets of German postilions, awoke a musical echo in the spacious streets through which we passed.'

Whereas La Garde rode inside, most of his fellow travellers, including ladies, preferred the half price seats and fresh air on top of the vehicle. This entailed clambering up a long ladder to the roof. It also required a strong head once they got there. For once they were perched aloft, they had to keep their balance all the time, even when asleep.

As the coach careered along at full speed, he observed from his comfortable seat that an inexperienced traveller clung to one end of the seat in a rigid state of terror, while at the other end the habitué balanced himself with the nonchalance of a sailor on a yardarm.

In fact La Garde was lucky enough to travel during the golden age of coaching, when the famous yellow and black mail coaches, their doors decorated with the Royal Arms, were among the most romantic sights of the English countryside. The coachmen were celebrated too; and every so often a swell from the old Four-in-Hand Club, such as the Marquis of Worcester or the Duke of Beaufort, would take over the reins. For instance the 'Age', immortalised in Herring's painting (and who knows how many Christmas cards) was regularly driven by Sir Vincent Cotton.

Very different it was from 50 years earlier, when two primitive vehicles left the Old Ship on alternate days and travelled via Chailey to the Swan with Two Necks in Lad Lane, or through Lewes and Uckfield to the Golden Cross Inn at Charing Cross. These were hardly more than waggons with a rumble tumble behind; and since the rear part had no springs were as pleasant to travel in, we are told, 'as if a man had been employed to kick one all the way from Brighton to London'. The only alternative—unless you

33. The 'Defiance' on Lewes Hill. The coach made regular runs from London to the Old Ship, Brighton via Tunbridge Wells and Lewes. The coach was painted yellow with a black top and the seats were upholstered in dark blue with a gold fringe. The body of the coach was embellished with paintings of the principal stopping places, including the Old Ship

34. A letter written by Carleton Blyth, the driver of the 'Defiance'. Carleton Blyth was one of the occupants of the coach 'Old Times' when it made its record-breaking run in 1888 from London to the Old Ship and back in 7 hours and 50 minutes

"Defiance" Coach.

St. James's Hotel.
Piccadilly.
3. Feb. 80.
Dear Mr. Bacon
Will you
give us Stabling
& Coach House room

if we pull up
at your House.
Yrs faithfully.
Carleton V. Blyth.

Mr. Bacon.
"Old Ship"

15. The Chain Pier

St Nicholas' Parish Church Brighton

16. St Nicolas's Church

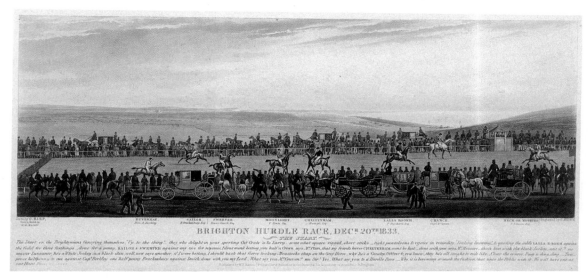

17. Brighton Hurdle Race, 1833

18. Two Bathing Beauties

hired a post chaise, or came in your own carriage—was a covered waggon which left London every Tuesday at 3 a.m. and arrived at Brighton on Thursday afternoon, having averaged about a mile an hour. Passengers who boarded it along the road (like Roderick Random and Strap, when they travelled to London) simply tumbled into the straw and made their peace as best they could with those already in residence.

But once Brighton became fashionable, and the Mail coaches were introduced in 1784, coaching began to develop into a lucrative business. Both John Hicks of the Old Ship and Shergold of the Castle were among the early promoters; within four years they and their partners were running eight stage coaches to London.

Even so Shergold felt bound to admit that they were hardly for the faint-hearted. More time on the journey was spent walking or drinking than actually riding, for at the bottom of each steep hill the coachman obliged all the passengers to go up on foot, 'it being absolutely killing to his horses', and since a great deal of business was transacted along the route by the coachmen, gin bottle in hand, no public house was passed without a mandatory halt.

Another account makes it all sound rather jolly. After leaving Lawrence Lane in the City at seven, the passengers had breakfast at 'The Cock' at Sutton at nine. 'The next stoppage for refreshment was at "The Tangier" (Banstead Downs), a rural little spot famous for its elderberry wine, which used to be brought from the cottage "roking hot", and, on a cold wintry morning, few refused to partake of it. George the Fourth invariably stopped here and took a glass from the hand of Miss Jeal as he sat in his carriage. The important business of luncheon took place at Reigate, where sufficient time was allowed the passengers to view the Barons' Cave. Handcross was the next resting place, celebrated for its "neat" liquors, the landlord of the Inn standing bottle-in-hand at the door. But the grand halt for dinner was made at Staplefield Common, celebrated for its famous black cherry trees, under the branches of which, when the fruit was ripe, the coaches were allowed to draw up and the passengers to partake of its tempting produce. The hostess of the hostelry here was famed for her rabbit puddings, which were always waiting the arrival of the coach, and to which the travellers never failed to do such ample justice that ordinarily they found it quite impossible to leave at the hour appointed; so grogs, pipes, and ale were ordered in, and, to use the language of the fraternity, "not a wheel wagged" for two hours. The coach then went on to Clayton Hill, and as the passengers had to walk up this ascent, a cup of tea was sometimes found to be necessary at Patcham, after which Brighton was safely reached by 7 p.m.'

In 1813 a service began running from Brighton to London and back the same evening, taking six hours each way, and within a few years some 62 coaches were on the road daily to various destinations. Some of them still left from the Old Ship, but the principal coach offices were now in Castle Square, which bustled at all hours with passengers and porters and hangers-on waiting to hear the latest news, for if there were any sensational tidings the London coaches would have them. During the trial of Queen Caroline, for instance, crowds lined the post-roads for reports of the proceedings to be shouted from the coachtops, and when the Reform Bill was being debated the latest intelligence from Parliament was broadcast by the coachmen or guards on the roof as the coach rushed past.

So, all spit and polish and gleaming in the sunshine, the coaches were drawn up in Castle Square. Covered with richly braided cloths, the teams of horses champed their bits and pawed the ground as if sharing the excitement of the scene. In due course the brightly-coated guards took their places, bugles in hand; with much ceremony the coachman mounted the box, tightened the ribbons and flourished his whip. Then, as the clock in the Pavilion tower struck, the horse-cloths were snatched away by the ostlers, the bugles sounded, and there was a shout 'Off she goes!'

Would the 'Red Rover' reach London in only $4\frac{1}{2}$ hours? Why not—one June day it did the trip in four hours and ten minutes. And though the railway was soon to put these stage-coaches out of business, not even the 'Brighton Belle' would ever match equipages like the 'Rover' or the 'Age' for sheer glamour of travel. No wonder that the 'Red Rover', lovingly restored by enthusiasts, was put back on the road in 1957 for a commemorative run. For this was the stuff of nostalgia, even if in modern traffic the trip took over ten hours.

CHAPTER 10

The Coming of the Railway

Sandwiched between the reigns of his brother and his niece, William IV's seven years on the throne were a time of transition—neither quite Georgian nor even Victorian, but a mixture of both: at once a postscript to the old order and a prelude to the new one. Perhaps the character of this kindly old monarch was illustrated (in Brighton eyes at least) by his recognition of Mrs Fitzherbert's position, and his fondness for that audacious feat of engineering, the Chain Pier.

Deeply distressed by the evidence of Maria's marriage certificate and the forbearance she had shown, the King would probably have made a public acknowledgement of her marriage, had Wellington not dissuaded him. Instead, he offered her the title of Duchess which—knowing how many King's mistresses had borne such a title—she refused to accept. But she did consent to go into Royal mourning for George IV, and to dress her servants in the Royal livery. From then onwards she was a frequent guest at the Pavilion, and her carriage, with its coachmen in scarlet, became a familiar sight in Brighton until her death in 1837. Each Saturday evening she went to make her confession at St John the Baptist's Church in Kemp Town, where it is said that the Irish priest instructed his waiting woman to bob her a curtsy: 'for maybe she's the rightful Queen of England—and maybe she's not!' The monument showing her kneeling in a penitential pose, with three wedding rings on her finger, can still be seen in the church.

Meanwhile 'Sailor William' continued to potter around the town as he had done for so many years, chatting with strangers and calling informally

35. The splendid Brighton viaduct was built in just ten months to carry the railway line from Brighton to Lewes. It has one central arch and 26 semicircular arches. Its graceful yet functional lines have been much admired and nearly 130 years later it is still in use. One thing which has changed is the landscape it traverses—now completely built up

36. *An event as important as the opening of the London to Brighton railway was a cause for celebration and provided the inspiration for this piece of music. The use of the word railroad instead of railway is interesting. The illustration gives us a good idea of the labour involved in carving out the station. The excavation of the chalk hillside was carried out by 3,500 navvies and 570 horses. The train is shown puffing towards the terminus designed by David Mocatta*

37. *All satin and pearls this delectable girl simply called* A Brighton Beauty *was drawn by A.E. Chalon and engraved by J. Thomson*

on friends. Wet or fine, he took his daily constitutional. Sometimes he walked on the cliffs. But usually he paced up and down the Chain Pier, which reminded him, he said, 'Of the most delightful place in the world—the deck of a ship.'

The pier was the first of its kind to have been constructed in England. Like a delicate bridge it stretched out into the sea, its chains suspended in graceful curves from four great tapering towers modelled on the gateways at Karnak. Built by a company formed at the Old Ship in 1822, it was erected in under twelve months to the design of Captain Samuel Brown RN, an expert in chain cables. Its purpose was to unload coal and merchandise, which hitherto had simply been dumped on the beach, but also to embark passengers on the steam packets that were beginning to ply between Brighton and Dieppe. Until then the sailing ships had been obliged to anchor out at sea more or less opposite the Old Ship, and travellers were conveyed to and fro in small punts. Frequently they had to be carried for the last few yards through the waves on the backs of fishermen or bathing attendants while their horses, carriages and belongings followed precariously on rafts.

Yet if the Chain Pier's facilities gave a significant boost to trade, its functional beauty hardly concorded with George IV's romantic visions. Musgrave tells us that when leaving Brighton in 1825 the King took a farewell drive along the sea front to survey this remarkable new structure. Though he gave no hint of his thoughts, it must have seemed to him to be the portent of an incomprehensible new world.

Could he have known, the tenor of life at the Pavilion was to change perceptibly too. For while William IV preferred a simple life—all he and the Queen desired, he used so often to repeat, was to be comfortable—he found that the Pavilion was ideal for entertaining; and curiously enough the state functions held there during his reign were more lavish than those given when his brother had been King. Mary Frampton remarked in 1831 that about 40 guests were invited every evening to dinners 'realising the ideas of the entertainments spoken of in the Arabian Nights'. Greville, who was present the following year at a council for the dissolution of Parliament, found the town very full, bustling, gay and amusing. 'Chesterfields, Howes, Lievens, Cowpers, all at Brighton, and plenty of occupation in visiting, gossiping, dawdling, riding and driving; a very idle life, impossible to do anything. The Court very active, vulgar and hospitable, King, Queen, Princes, Princesses and bastards constantly trotting about in every direction.'

Their Majesties invited such mobs to dinner, chuckled the wit and politician Joseph Jekyll, that he mistook the arrivals at Margate for the list of their guests. And as a matter of fact, he was not far wrong. For every morning the Old Ship and the Albion were asked to send their lists of arrivals to the Pavilion so that at breakfast the King could mark the names of those to be invited that evening.

On the other hand the Queen was already setting Victorian standards. No décolleté gowns were permitted, and ladies who once complained that they could not exhibit enough bosom for the late King now had to muffle themselves up to the chin. Nor would Queen Adelaide receive anyone of whom she disapproved. Old Lady Aldborough, who loved to relate the

187

38. A triumphal archway erected for the visit of Queen Victoria to Brighton in 1841. Notice the large advertisement for Shuckard's ale and beer—Leonard Shuckard was one-time manager of the Old Ship Hotel

more titillating exploits of her adventurous past, and the Duchess of St Albans were among those she barred. 'You know that the Queen would not let old mother St Albans come to her ball at the Pavilion, tho' there were 830 people' wrote Creevey.

Yet for all the splendour, William IV was no gourmet; and former habitués of the Pavilion noticed a sad deterioration in the royal cuisine. 'What a change to be sure,' Lord Dudley was heard muttering one evening, 'Cold pâtés and hot champagne.' Nor was it unknown for the King to indulge in ward-room activities. On New Year's Eve 1833 he jumped up as the clock struck twelve and insisted on having a country dance, recounts John Crocker. 'Lady Falkland sat down to the piano and struck up a lively tune. Everyone took out their partners, and who do you think the King took out? Lord Amelius Beauclerk! The sight of the King and the old admiral going down the middle hand in hand was the most royally extravagant farce that was ever seen.'

Although the boisterous old monarch was the kindliest of men, much given to buying children sweets at the little shops on the pier, he nourished a deep aversion for his sister-in-law, the Duchess of Kent. Consequently neither she nor her daughter were ever invited to the Pavilion, and the first time Queen Victoria came to Brighton was four months after her accession.

To welcome her on her arrival, the North Gate was turned into a triumphal arch covered with flowers, and she was escorted into the town by 200 gentlemen on horseback, all sporting purple sashes. Creevey, who had surveyed her uncles with distaste for years, thought her a homely little thing. 'She laughs in real earnest, opening her mouth as wide as it can go, showing not very pretty gums. She eats as heartily as she laughs. I think I

Pic Nic at the Beach Hotel

39. *Cartoons such as this one poked fun at the hordes of day trippers who descended on Brighton after the construction of the railway. Unfamiliar with the vagaries of the sea, this unfortunate family watch as their picnic is swept away. All the same Brighton became the 'lungs of the great capital' and many a Londoner enjoyed the bracing air after weeks in stuffy London*

may say she gobbles. She blushes and laughs every instant in so natural a way as to disarm everybody.' That evening the dome of the Music Room rang with her pure, clear voice as she sang an aria from an opera by da Costa.

Unfortunately such youthful exuberance could not last for long. If her first months on the throne were a sort of girlish Regency—an innocent harking back to the eighteenth century—it soon became clear that the times were changing. By the time she married her earnest Prince Albert, the Queen had become unmistakably Victorian.

And clearly her uncle's pleasure palace was not to her taste. 'The Pavilion is a strange odd Chinese-looking thing, both inside and outside', she wrote in her Journal. Pleasant though it was to have Lord Melbourne explain state affairs as they rode up and down the front, she could not get over the feeling that the whole place was tainted by association with her wicked uncles. Nor could she become reconciled to its lack of privacy. Moreover, it became apparent that Prince Albert disliked it too. The people were indiscreet and troublesome. As *Punch* said: 'a set of unmannerly curs that poke their noses under the bonnet of a Queen' whenever she chose to go walking on the pier.

Unamused by such attentions, Victoria swept off to the railway station behind a troop of dragoons, and did not return to Brighton for the next 20 years. It was noted, however, that her abhorrence for the Pavilion did not extend to its contents, since 143 van-loads of furniture, carpets, porcelain and paintings were promptly removed to Buckingham Palace and Windsor Castle.

A period in history was ending. For if the Queen had become Victorian, so had the age. As the polite scepticism of previous days became submerged beneath the industrial credos of Birmingham and Manchester (not to mention the strict morality of Evangelists and Nonconformists) the railway station and the pulpit began to replace the Pavilion as the centres of Brighton life. For a hundred years the town had grown up under the influence of a charming but supercilious aristocracy. From now on it would reflect the tastes of yeomen who had become manufacturers, of shopkeepers who had grown into wholesalers—in short of a whole new hierarchy recognised by its contemporaries as 'thoughtful, manly-minded, conscious of duty and obligation', along with a multitude of happy-go-lucky trippers who were still unblushingly described as 'the lower orders'.

Above all, transport facilities had improved beyond measure since the beginning of the century when Cruikshank amused himself with fantasies revolving around 'the miraculous power of steam'. Only two years after the local solicitor William James published a pamphlet setting out the advantages of an 'engine rail-road' linking London to Brighton, a company was formed at the Old Ship to develop such a project, while a town meeting held in the same premises decided in favour of building an iron railway to transport coal between Brighton and Shoreham. This was in 1825, the year that the world's first public railway opened between Stockton and Darlington. In fact little came of these schemes at the time, or indeed of John Rennie's proposal to construct a line from London to Bristol by way of Brighton. People still preferred the brightly-coloured stage-coaches to ugly 'billies' puffing filthy clouds of steam over the countryside.

True, a number of steam coaches began to do the Brighton trip, but the novelty of being drawn by a four wheeled road locomotive rather than by four splendidly caprisoned horses soon palled. Romance was lacking in a vehicle which 'compared unfavourably for beauty with a prison van', and in any case the frequent stops necessary for refuelling made them no faster than the glamorous 'Red Rover'.

Inexorably, however, the railways began to throw their tentacles throughout the country, and after an exhaustive Parliamentary inquiry work on the Brighton railway finally started in July 1838 with the great cutting through the north Downs at Merstham. In the days before bulldozers this was a huge project, carried out by hundreds of navvies who lifted the soil up the steep slopes in wheel-barrows. It was done, says the railway historian Terry Coleman, by barrow runs—a spectacular and dangerous procedure. 'A rope attached to the barrow and also to each man's belt, ran up the side of the cutting, and then around a pulley at the top, where it was attached to a horse. When the barrow was loaded, a signal was given to the horse-driver at the top, and the man was drawn up the side of the cutting, balancing the barrow in front of him. If the horse pulled steadily and the man kept his balance, everything went well. The man tipped his barrow-load on top of the cutting, turned round and went down the side of the cutting again, this time drawing his barrow after him, while the horse all the time kept the rope taut and took most of the weight of the empty

40. The Brighton to Shoreham Railway was opened on 11 May 1840. Although there was only room for 230 select passengers on the first run, there were plenty of spectators on hand to view this historic event. The general air of festivity was enhanced by the band of the 12th Lancers playing popular music. In the evening the satisfied directors and their guests sat down to an elaborate dinner at the Old Ship, Brighton

barrow.' More than 6,000 men and nearly 1,000 horses, helped by five locomotives, were needed to build the five tunnels, 99 bridges, and the 37 arched viaducts that carried the Brighton line a hundred feet above the valley of the Ouse south of Balcombe. These nomadic swarms of 'land-navigators', many of them Irishmen who had come over originally to construct the canals, worked 70 hours a week and earned twice as much as ordinary labourers. Not surprisingly, they terrorised the Sussex countryside with their drunken 'randies', causing all but the local inn-keepers to retire behind bolted doors.

The Shoreham branch was the first part of the Brighton line to be completed, and in May 1840 an inaugural trainload of 230 bigwigs made the return journey in just under half an hour (despite a hitch on departure when the carriage brakes were left on). That evening the Directors threw a splendid dinner at the Old Ship, where 15 years previously the project had been conceived; but the real celebrations took place 14 months later when the full line was opened. It had taken three years to build at a cost of more than £2 million.

Almost the whole population of Brighton gathered on the warm sunny afternoon of 21 September 1841 to witness the arrival of the first train from London, reports the *Herald*. A cloud of steam from the mouth of the Patcham tunnel heralded the long black train with its ten carriages; the band of the Scots Greys played the National Anthem as it slid into the station. Later, thousands of people crowded into the makeshift station (its great arched roof of glass supported by surprisingly slender cast iron columns was not built until much later), while this time the Directors of the railroad company and their friends were the guests of the town. A banquet for 200 persons was held at the Old Ship (at £1 11s 6d a cover) which included turbot, game, venison, joints, champagne and congratu-

latory speeches. ('Brighton is now on the grand route between London and Paris, and will become the direct communication between the two great capitals of the greatest Kingdoms on earth.')

Even if such laudatory sentiments were hardly fulfilled, the railway superseded the stage-coach with astonishing speed. True, Macaulay the historian, travelling from London to Paris by way of Brighton in 1843, was by no means enchanted with the journey, which took 20¾ hours. In fact he described it with a series of groans. Groan one was a packed carriage with a sick lady smelling of ether, a healthy gentleman smelling of brandy, the thermometer 102° in the shade, and himself not in the shade. The effect of which was that his white trousers were scorched into a pair of very service-nankeens. (i.e. buff-coloured). Since Macaulay probably travelled first class in a carriage with well padded seats, as opposed to second (hard seats) or third (open sides, but with a roof) or fourth which didn't have a roof, and the trip to Brighton took only two hours, one must assume that the British propensity for grumbling has not changed much in the last century and a half. Nor the trains, come to that, give or take a class or two.

Possibly he had boarded a stopping train, for the expresses covered the distance in an hour and 45 minutes. They were often limited to first class. Even so, it was far quicker than by coach, and cheaper too. Whereas an outside seat on the coach cost 13s, a second class ticket on the train was priced at 9s 6d. Moreover, as rail fares progressively diminished, and cheap day excursion tickets were introduced—in 1845 a third class Sunday return cost 5s, in 1849 3s 6d, in 1861 half a crown—the volume of traffic increased dramatically. Without any doubt the coming of the railway marked the beginning of the modern age for Brighton. By 1861 the annual number of visitors topped 250,000, and on Easter Monday alone 132,000 people came down by train. Even if the Chairman of the railway company was over-optimistic in forecasting that Brighton would become the link

41. This steel engraving by T. Jeavons was executed from a drawing by R.H. Nibbs c.1846. Note the old oak railings on the promenade which were replaced in the 1880s by the cast iron ones we are familiar with today

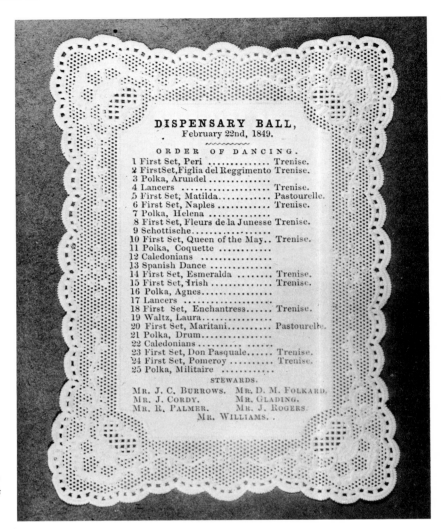

DISPENSARY BALL,
February 22nd, 1849.

ORDER OF DANCING.

1 First Set, Peri .... Trenise.
2 First Set, Figlia del Reggimento Trenise.
3 Polka, Arundel ....
4 Lancers .... Trenise.
5 First Set, Matilda............ Pastourelle.
6 First Set, Naples .... Trenise.
7 Polka, Helena ....
8 First Set, Fleurs de la Junesse Trenise.
9 Schottische.................
10 First Set, Queen of the May.. Trenise.
11 Polka, Coquette ....
12 Caledonians ....
13 Spanish Dance ....
14 First Set, Esmeralda .... Trenise.
15 First Set, Irish .... Trenise.
16 Polka, Agnes................
17 Lancers ....
18 First Set, Enchantress...... Trenise.
19 Waltz, Laura ....
20 First Set, Maritani.......... Pastourelle.
21 Polka, Drum...............
22 Caledonians ....
23 First Set, Don Pasquale...... Trenise.
24 First Set, Pomeroy .... Trenise.
25 Polka, Militaire ....

STEWARDS.

MR. J. C. BURROWS.   MR. D. M. FOLKARD,
MR. J. CORDY.   MR. GLADING.
MR. R. PALMER.   MR. J. ROGERS.
MR. WILLIAMS. .

42. *A programme daintily edged with paper lace for a Ball held at the Old Ship in 1849 for the funds of the new Dispensary in Queen's Road*

between London and Paris, his confidence that 'the traffic coming to Brighton would be very superior and transform it into the first watering place in the kingdom' was thoroughly justified.

His hosts at that memorable dinner were Edward Cuff and John Strachan, to whom William Attree's son Thomas had leased the Old Ship in 1834 for an annual rental of £604, though as a matter of fact the contract did not include all the buildings involved. For one thing the coach house and stables were already held by a coal merchant called James Phippen on a 21-year lease at £90 per annum. Furthermore, the property on the east corner of Ship Street—including those cosy Regency drawing rooms from which we have been viewing the Brighton scene—belonged to yet a different landlord and were subject to a separate lease at £100 a year. And at the same time Cuff and Strachan had permission to build an extension on the side of these premises which cost them a further £100 in ground rent. What with one thing and another it was all as involved as any modern lease, and Judy Middleton points out that 'the contract had several strings attached because it was stipulated that within 18 months some of the structure must be taken down and rebuilt, and that £1,300 must be expended on the work, bills being produced if required. As regards maintenance the stonework, woodwork, and ironwork must be painted every third year. There was also a restriction on use, for the building was to be used solely as a lodging house for the accommodation of persons resorting to the Old Ship. Should Cuff and Strachan attempt to hold an auction on the premises they would incur a penalty of £200. Lastly, and perhaps remembering Hicks' difficulties as a cautionary tale, the building must on no account be mortgaged'. Bearing in mind the difficulties antiquarians have in dating these hugger-mugger buildings, this seems to suggest that the drawing rooms were redecorated in their present 'regency' style around 1835.

Since the Old Ship remained, for nearly 150 years, so much a family affair, it is intriguing to trace the relationship of the dramatis personae. For a start Edward Cuff's father, old John Jackson Cuff, originally the proprietor of a tavern in London, had the customary clutch of daughters. Of these, Caroline married John Strachan, her brother's partner; and in due course two other daughters moved to the centre of the stage as their husbands became involved in running the hotel. They were Mary Anne Cuff, who became the wife of Samuel Ridley, the auctioneer; and Charlotte Frances, the youngest of the Cuff daughters, who married Robert Bacon.

Robert, who was to become such a notable figure in Victorian Brighton, was born in 1809 to a family of hoteliers. His father ran the Piercy Coffee House in Covent Garden, a well-known haunt of theatrical folk in the eighteenth century; two of his brothers were involved with the Freemason's Tavern in Great Queen Street, and a Bacon was mine host at one of England's oldest inns, the Black Boy at Chelmsford. So it ran in the family. By the early 1840s Robert Bacon was managing the Queen's Hotel in Birmingham when he began, as they said in those days, to pay his addresses to Charlotte Cuff, then a young lady of 18. His love letters, smelling faintly of sandalwood from the box in which they have been preserved, show him to have been a jealous and sentimental suitor, often irked by Charlotte's apparent coolness. But they were married in 1848, the year that her father died.

Before his death Cuff had bought out Thomas Attree's interest in the Old Ship, and there may have been some conflict of interest between his heirs, for in 1851 the property was put up for sale by auction at Garroway's Coffee House in London. Samuel Ridley and Robert Bacon instructed their agent Daniel Cronin to bid for them, and oddly enough it was knocked down to him for the paltry sum of £100. However the contents were valued at £7,527 14s 0d, of which the vendors accepted £5,000 in cash, the balance to be paid off in three years.

If Ridley and Robert Bacon were now joint owners of the Old Ship, it is apparent that Ridley (who had political aspirations and ended up as an alderman) was simply a sleeping partner. Though their association lasted for 36 years, it was Robert Bacon and his brother Arthur who ran the hotel.

With the business in their blood, this admirable team increased the Old Ship's reputation for good food, geniality and old-fashioned comfort against the competition of larger establishments such as the Bedford, the

43. *Charlotte Frances Bacon (1830–1910) was the youngest of eight children and her father John Jackson Cuff was former lessee of the Old Ship. She married Robert Bacon in 1848 when she was 18 years old and her bridegroom approaching forty*

44. *Robert Bacon (1809–1888) bought the Old Ship in 1851 in partnership with his brother-in-law, Samuel Ridley*

45. One of the best-known cricket prints ever produced depicts a cricket match between Sussex and Kent on the Level at Brighton with St Peter's Church prominent in the background. The match never actually took place but the people are real enough. There are 72 of them and each man had to have his portrait taken which accounts for the six years the picture was in preparation before it was finished in 1849. Note the top hats of the players but no gloves or pads. There are three Sussex players of particular note. F. W. Lillywhite (Nonpareil) is about to bowl—in later years it was recorded he took 685 wickets in three seasons. Tom Box is behind the wicket (a handsome man until a cricket ball smashed his nose at Lord's) and for a remarkable period of 24 years he played for Sussex at every match. John Wisden (dressed in white) stands on the left of the recumbent figure in the foreground; one of the finest all-round cricketers which Brighton has produced, his name is remembered today with the production of Wisden Cricketer's Almanac

York, the Albion—and, in due course, the spanking new Grand Hotel which, with its glamorous white continental aspect, opened in 1864. Undoubtedly the Bacon brothers' success owed as much to their personalities as to their attention to detail. Soon as well known in London as on the coast, their name became synonymous with the Old Ship: while Robert Bacon was described as 'that Prince of caterers', the cheerful Arthur, with his long flowing locks, became 'our local Beau Brummell'. Tributes to their hospitality were voiced by such eminent contemporaries as Dickens, Harrison Ainsworth, Sala and Thackeray. These literary figures, along with a host of other notable guests, enjoyed the ministrations of Miss Louise Bauer, who was manageress for many years before retiring 'to enter into the holy bonds of matrimony' and the headwaiter, Carl Edouard Finger, known universally as Louis.

A single quote will suffice: 'Men who know what's what, and like things plain and good, go to Mr Robert Bacon's far-famed hostelry, The Old Ship, which literary men generally, and the versatile George Augustus Sala in particular, have deservedly popularised as one of the institutions of London-super-mare.'

CHAPTER 11

Mattins and Mutton's

Sala, that most celebrated of Victorian journalists, used to stress that the Brighton of his youth had essentially been a royal domain.

'When Royalty finally abandoned the town,' he recalls, 'there was a general consensus of opinion that Brighton was ruined, and would never recover from the social blow it had received.'

But, he went on to observe, people had forgotten that the railway was coming. It came, and the fortunes of Brighton were immediately restored. The population increased by leaps and bounds and the town grew as if by magic. 'Rich merchants and stockbrokers discovered that the propinquity of Brighton to London made it exceptionally elegible as a place of residence for gentlemen who went up to town in the morning on business and could return in time for dinner. Thus Brighton became the permanent home of a numerous and affluent class of residents, whose patronage was quite as beneficial to the trade of the town as that of the aristocracy had been.'

The age of the commuter had dawned. Yet even if Lombard Street and Mincing Lane were taking over, the aristocracy was still in evidence. For instance the Sixth Duke of Devonshire—the Bachelor Duke as he was known—entertained widely and lavishly at his house in Kemp Town. A sufferer from asthma, he loved the Brighton climate and thought that the dining room on the first floor of No 1 Lewes Crescent, which caught all the sun, was the best place in the world. And his sister, Lady Granville, regarded Kemp Town as 'a little kingdom of one's own'.

Two of Europe's most prominent leaders, who had been overthrown in

46. *Nowadays Sussex people associate November 5th Bonfire celebrations exclusively with Lewes but in days past the scene was equally as lively at Brighton. As can be seen from the illustration, the festivities were somewhat rough with blazing tar-barrels rolling through the crowd, lighted torches and bonfires (note the absence of female faces). The Brighton fishermen believed that shoals of herring which arrived off the coast at that time of year were attracted inshore by the light of the bonfires*

47. Fireworks erupt over the Chain Pier to celebrate the Treaty of Paris in 1856. This brought the Crimean War to an end in which some 45,000 British soldiers died, largely through disease and inadequate supplies rather than through enemy action. The Earl of Cardigan, the popular hero of the Charge of the Light Brigade, had once rented a house at Hove while his regiment, the 11th Hussars, was quartered at Preston Barracks

the revolutions of 1848, must have echoed these thoughts as they took refuge in Brighton. Escaping with his family from Dieppe to Newhaven, King Louis-Philippe of France spent some time as the guest of the Marquess of Bristol in Sussex Gardens before settling in Hastings. While Prince Metternich, the great Austrian statesman who had been regarded as 'The Master of Europe', spent the winter of 1848 quietly at No 42 Brunswick Terrace, from whose windows (he wrote enthusiastically) 'The immensity of the sea charms the eye.'

Even in late November, the climate delighted him. 'I now know of no healthier place than Brighton. The air is pure, the temperature is extraordinarily mild and I know of no spot in the northern latitudes which unites so favourably those conditions of existence that one finds in the Midi. You have only to look at the vegetation to be confirmed in this opinion.' In a garden nearby was a magnolia tree every bit as fine as the one in his villa on Lake Como. 'Anywhere the plants of the Midi do well in the open air is a good place to live. If, on top of that, the country is quiet and peaceful, then all the better!'

Contrary to expectations, these years marked the beginning of the *most fashionable era in the history of the town* (surely the judgement of Brighton's own historian should be printed in italics) outdoing even Regency times in displays of wealth and the pursuit of pleasure. 'The number of splendid carriages and coaches, always a symbol of affluence in Victorian days as

much as motor cars are in our own, was greatly increased, and the carriage processions along the seafront were an important feature of the social programme.'

There were nuances, of course. The fashionable season began in the first week of October and lasted until a little after Christmas, resuming over Easter. 'Between three and five o'clock the Front is crowded with barouches, landaus, broughams, mail-phaetons and dog-carts' wrote Sala. 'It must be a very inclement October and November in Brighton if the great majority of the landaus and barouches are not open.'

In the morning, the ladies turned out on horseback, and children on ponies, while gentlemen strolled along to their clubs. Of these there were several. The Union, on the Kings Road above the Bedford Hotel was noted for its luncheons; the New Club for its billiards. The Orleans Residential, which attracted members of White's along with the aristocratic, military, artistic and literary community, was considered the smartest. Moreover, its coffee-room was open to ladies.

Dinner parties were held every night, and the Theatre Royal was crowded. There were dramatic recitals, concerts at the Old Ship, lectures at the Dome, a sequence of public and private balls. Perhaps the most dazzling of these was a grand Fancy Dress Ball given in the Old Ship Assembly Rooms by Mr Morrell Dorington Longden, a flamboyant character who sought to recapture the magnificence of the ancient Assyrian court at Nineveh, which Layard, the archaeologist, had recently brought to light.

48. A lively scene on Brighton beach on 8 August 1857, where a number of fashionably dressed visitors are about to embark on a short sea trip. The boat may well have been the Skylark—the first of a succession of these famous boats bearing the same name having arrived at Brighton in 1852. In the background two fishing boats, which had reached the end of their sailing days, have been cut in half and up-ended against the cliff to serve as huts for storing nets and tackle

111

49. Captain Fred Collins was a popular local character who spent almost 60 years around the sea-front. He was the owner of the famous Skylark pleasure boats and probably the originator of the catch-phrase 'Any more for the Skylark?' In 1880 an hour's trip cost one shilling. His headgear was invariably a dark hard-glazed straw boater

50. Sea-bathing was a serious affair—you were not expected to enjoy the experience necessarily. The ladies bathing from machines were assisted by 'dippers'—stalwart Brighton females who seemed to take a perverse delight in their charges' timidity at the sight of the waves

'Having travelled abroad a great deal and contracted a taste for Continental decorative art, Mr Longden gave his fancy full play' wrote the *Brighton Herald*. 'At the north end of the Telemachus Room was a scarlet dais and golden throne alluded to in Layard's Nineveh as used by the Assyrian Kings. The drapery of it was embroidered with gold, being thrown carelessly over the back; and the whole was surmounted by a light azure-coloured canopy fringed with gold. On each side of the throne was a scarlet banneret bearing the "winged bull"; and the dais was flanked on each side by a magnificent display of flowers.' When the guests arrived, they were received by Mr Longden enthroned in the character of Sardanapalus, and so gorgeously costumed, so voluptuously jewelled was their host that even Prinny would have been hard put to compete with him.

But in summer the scene changed completely as Brighton became a suburb of the metropolis. Summer meant bathing and eating winkles on the beach. For the children, it also meant driving in goat-chaises; sand-castles, sea-weed and shells, not to mention the excitements of the pier. The West Pier, which opened in 1866 opposite Regency Square (to the great annoyance of its residents) was celebrated for its side-shows, and on Sundays over 10,000 people would pass through the turnstiles. Later on, a huge concert hall was added, along with performing fleas. During the summer months, Brighton was rumbustiously vulgar.

Literary figures abounded. Thackeray, a frequent visitor during the 1840s, found the place irresistible—'gay and gaudy, like a harlequin's jacket.' Parts of *Vanity Fair*, which he had originally entitled *Pen and Pencil Sketches of English Society*, were written at the Old Ship, whither Thackeray dispatched his protagonists for their honeymoons on the eve of the Battle of Waterloo to 'enjoy themselves in great comfort and quietude . . .' (Though he slipped up by causing Lady Southdown to reside in Brunswick Square a full decade before it was built.) Later on, having got into the habit of taking furnished accommodation for himself and his family—usually at No 62 East Street, but also in Grand Parade and once at the corner of Marine

19. Lewes Crescent

20. The West Pier, illustrated on cover of the 'Brighton Quadrilles'

Square—he was often to be seen at the literary foregatherings held at 21 Sillwood Place by Eliza and Rosalind, the unmarried daughters of the novelist Horace Smith. In 1851 he gave his lectures on 'The Four Georges', those remarkable diatribes against the Hanoverians and in particular George IV,[1] which delighted American audiences but so infuriated Sir Osbert Sitwell. When asked by Henry Martin why they were held at the Town Hall rather than in the Pavilion itself, Thackeray adroitly replied that he 'did not like to abuse a man in his own house'.

Another devotee was Charles Dickens, who moved over from Broadstairs and became a regular visitor to Brighton for more than 30 years, alternating between the Old Ship and the Bedford Hotel.[2] It was at Brighton that he wrote the greater part of both *Bleak House* and *Dombey and Son*. While letters addressed to his publisher from the Old Ship are still to be seen (signed with the pen-name Boz), part of the action in *Dombey and Son* took place in the Bedford, and Harrison Ainsworth always believed that Dr Blimber's academy, to which young Paul Dombey was sent, was modelled on a private school in Chichester Terrace. But Dickens surely endeared himself to local residents with those readings from his works in the Old Ship Assembly Rooms and the Town Hall, which drew audiences of over a thousand at a time, and he 'found that peculiar personal relation between my audience and myself on which I counted most'.[3]

A subtle transition into the realms of the theatre! And to be sure the stage was well represented in Brighton. Indeed most of the famous actors and actresses of the day performed at the Theatre Royal, which since 1806 had enjoyed a special position in the theatrical world. No provincial theatre had a more metropolitan style or played to more fashionable audiences. Sarah Siddons—the 'Queen of Tragedy', Mrs Jordan, the Kean brothers, Joseph Grimaldi, William Macready and Madame Vestris were among the names that appeared on its playbills. What's more, when Jenny Lind, the Swedish soprano who had taken Covent Garden by storm, sang at the Town Hall, a locomotive was named after her. Though it might be construed as a dubious honour, a whole series of famous engines running on the Brighton line were known thereafter as 'Jenny Linds'.

A few years later Robert Bacon backed the actor-manager, Nye Chart, when he bought the Theatre Royal. Due to this connection most of the

Sir Henry Irving

Charles Dickens

William Makepeace Thackeray

1. 'But this George, what was he? I look through all his life and recognise but a bow and a grin.'

2. Dickens and his illustrator Charles Leech had an alarming experience when they rented a house together in 1849. Hardly were the two families installed at 16, Lansdowne Place than their landlord and his daughter went insane. 'If you could have heard the cursing and crying of the two; could have seen the physician and nurse quoited out into the passage by the madman at the hazard of their lives; could have seen Leech and me flying to the Doctor's rescue, could have seen our wives pulling us back . . .' Dickens wrote to a friend, who could readily understand why they had moved so hurriedly to the Bedford Hotel.

3. Speaking of audiences, a friend of Thackeray and Dickens wrote one of the most popular poems of the age, the now forgotten epic Orion, while staying at Brighton in 1843. It was Richard Henry Horne's publicity stunt of selling it for a farthing a copy that earned the poem instant if ephemeral fame, and Horne the title of 'Farthing Poet'. Later the poem's one immortal line, 'T'is always morning somewhere in the world' was inscribed on the sundial of the West Pier.

51. A grand Ball given by the officers of the 9th Lancers at the Royal Pavilion in 1863. In 1850 the Pavilion had been purchased from Queen Victoria by Brighton for £53,000. But it was an empty shell, all the furnishings and fittings having been removed. The first task was to refurbish the place and, fortunately, by 1863 Queen Victoria had agreed to return some of the larger chandeliers

theatrical folk became personal friends of the family and made the Old Ship their home. From Drury Lane Heinrich Jackson addressed letters to his 'beloved Bacon', while George Leitch amused himself writing to 'the round Bacons, the streaky Bacons, and you yourself'. Sadly most of the long line of once famous names who gave a great deal of pleasure to a great many people—one thinks of Ada Cavendish, who enjoyed a huge success in the United States, George Reeves Smith and the comedian J.L. Toole—are now quite forgotten. But Sir Henry Irving, at least, has joined the immortals.

One of his superstitions was that it brought him luck to walk to the theatre on the first night, and the Old Ship was handy for this purpose. Yet it did not save his opening appearance as Hamlet from being panned by the local critics. 'With all due deference to Mr Irving's histrionic power,' sniffed the *Brighton Gazette*, 'we cannot help feeling a certain amount of dissatisfaction, both with his elocutional ability and his interpretation of Hamlet'.

And this of the same Hamlet that became a cult in London and brought him a standing ovation in Dublin! Lord Tennyson thought it the greatest he had ever seen. Fortunately Irving's subsequent offerings with the Lyceum Company—a melodrama called *The Bells* and a tear-jerker entitled *Charles I*—got a better press in Brighton. Both were popular evergreens in his repertoire (*The Bells* was a favourite with Queen Victoria, who also had some reservations about Irving's elocution but considered him 'gentlemanly'). Later on, when Ellen Terry acted with Irving, she used to say she always

cried too much during the last scene of *Charles I* because Sir Henry's rendering of the part was so dignified and moving.

One of Irving's closest friends was the immensely popular Toole, whose famous opening line 'I hope I don't intrude' was always the signal for rapturous applause. It was Charles Dickens who first encouraged Toole to make a career on the stage, and once when playing the part of Bob Cratchit in *A Christmas Carol* he found himself participating in a somewhat Dickensian situation.

At each performance, Toole carved a real goose on the stage and served steamy plum-puddings to Mrs Cratchit and the seven little Cratchits, including Tiny Tim. Enormous helpings were always dished out, yet Toole was amazed to find that no matter how much was piled on to Tiny Tim's plate it always ended up empty. He decided to keep an eye on the little girl who took the part and sat on a low stool by the fireplace. He then discovered that the child was slipping the food through the fireplace to her little sister behind, so that the whole family—her father was a scene-shifter—enjoyed a huge supper every night. When Dickens heard the story he told Toole he should have given her all the goose.

Towards the end of his life, when he was already partially paralysed, Toole stayed at the Old Ship for months at a time. He felt at home in its friendly atmosphere, and was usually to be found in the smoking room to the right of the hall. He was treated like royalty. Streams of friends came to visit him every evening, but no one ever presumed to leave before Toole decided it was time to retire. Then the whole company rose, and, leaning on a friend's arm, the old campaigner would hobble out, shaking hands and saying a few words to each person. So encyclopaedic was his knowledge of

52. *Charles Dickens was a frequent visitor to Brighton where he stayed at the Old Ship or the Bedford. This painting by C.W. Nicholls is called* What are the Wild Waves Saying? *and is based on* Dombey and Son *which is partially set in Brighton. The little invalid Paul Dombey was modelled on Dickens' crippled nephew. Young Dombey attends Dr Blimber's Academy at Brighton whose hot-house cramming proves too much for him. Paul dies quite early on in the book but throughout his short life he seemed old for his age and was obsessed by what the waves were trying to tell him*

53. King's Road, Brighton, Old
Ship Hotel and West Pier,
photographed by Edward Fox in
May 1867

the theatre that it was rare for an actor to be introduced to him without
Toole being able to make some appropriate comment on his work.

By the fireside he would exchange reminiscences with Beerbohm Tree,
that fastidious actor-manager whose sumptuous Shakespearean productions
featured real fountains and spectacular crowd scenes; or with Sir Julius
Benedict (best remembered for *The Lily of Killarney*) who had written the
music for Irving's *Romeo & Juliet* in 1882— though Toole gently poked fun
at Irving and Ellen Terry for taking the parts of young lovers at their age.
And he would chuckle with Madame Emma Albani over the incident at
Covent Garden when one of her admirers had been so moved by her singing
that he threw a box on to the stage containing a diamond pendant. In the
excitement of the moment his aim was unfortunate. The box hit her
squarely on the forehead as she stooped to pick up the bouquets that were
strewn all over the stage, practically knocking her out and causing the
audience to rise to its feet in alarm, imagining that an attempt had been
made on her life.

By such vivid characters was the mystique of the Brighton stage main-
tained, even if Nye Chart had a tendency to play the leading roles at the
Theatre Royal himself. When he died in 1875 his widow, herself one of the
most popular actresses of the day, took control and to the Royal's play-
boards were added such legendary names as Mrs Patrick Campbell, Sarah
Bernhardt, the Kendals, Seymour Hicks, George Giddens and Matheson
Lang. On Thursday afternoons the entire company of a West End play
would come down to Brighton for a 'flying matinee'; while her Christmas
pantomimes became a forcing ground for future stars.

Another popular venue was Wright's Music Hall, later known as the
Oxford, where Sir Charles Cochran made his stage debut. And in the latter
part of the nineteenth century one of the most popular places of entertainment was the Royal Hippodrome, originally built as a permanent home for
Ginnett's Circus, which came over from France during the Franco-Prussian
war. Subsequently, as the Gaiety, it specialised in melodrama, with shows

54. A crowded scene on the King's Road in 1879. Note the children having a ride in the little goat-cart and the crocodile of young ladies taking their constitutional. With its healthy climate, Brighton was considered an ideal place for schools

full of blood-curdling thrills and suspense (in one of them, two trains thundered past each other on the stage). But once Al Jolson brought the silver screen to maturity with the prophetic words 'You ain't heard nothing yet' (which the 40th President of the USA transposed to such good effect 56 years later) the days of the music hall were numbered. Even the second Hippodrome in Middle Street, which started as a skating rink, was doomed to end up as a Bingo hall.

High Bohemia, it must be said, almost rubbed shoulders with a world we know chiefly from Dickens. Just around the corner from the Theatre Royal, in the vicinity of Church Street, was an area where blasphemy and black eyes abounded. 'Go there any night' says the guide book 'and you will see hideous old women, drunken old men, young men and mere boys hopelessly intoxicated, reeling and staggering in the road.' Such scenes, though commonplace enough in mid-Victorian towns, may help to account for the large number of churches erected at Brighton during this period— most of which were built by a remarkable family, the Wagners.

The Rev. Henry Wagner was vicar for 46 years. An autocratic High Churchman, he treated the town as if it were a private fief, lavishing the large fortune he had inherited from his father (who had been hatter to George II) on the parish with such benevolent despotism that his incumbency was described, somewhat ruefully, by the Bishop of Chichester as 'a bishopric within a bishopric'. It was Henry Wagner who footed the bill for St Paul's Church in West Street, where the liturgy introduced by his son Arthur soon became so ritualistic, the vestments so colourful and the music so choral, that the services became known as 'the Sunday opera at St Paul's'.

Yet the younger Wagner was also impelled by a missionary zeal. 'It is a testimony to the religious dedication of Arthur Wagner in carrying Christi-

55. *Brighton College was founded in 1847 to provide an education of the highest order for the sons of noblemen and gentlemen. Nineteen architects competed for the privilege of designing the new school and George Gilbert Scott was chosen. The ornate gateway was added some 40 years later. It was designed by T. G. Jackson who had trained in Scott's office and moreover was an Old Brightonian. The gateway is a marvel of Victorian detail*

56. *These sketches at Brighton were executed in 1885. The inset of a man smoking his clay pipe is captioned 'A Brighton native!' The round inset shows a young lady with a novel fashion—flowers pinned to her fur tippet. The children playing croquet and battledore and shuttlecock are in Preston Park which covers an area of 62 acres and was opened in 1884*

anity into the slums of Brighton that the first two churches built at his own expense should have been, not great masterpieces of grandeur and beauty like his father's church St Paul's, or his later churches St Bartholomew's and St Martin's,' comments Musgrave, 'but two humble mission churches, St Mary and St Magdalene's, and the Church of the Annunciation, built two years later.' What's more, the Rev. Wagner acted as his own whipper-in. He would summon people to St Mary's by striding round the neighbouring streets ringing a handbell.

Another man of God, writing under the pseudonym of Cuthbert Bede, sought to blend the worlds of fashion and faith in a popular novel entitled *Mattins and Mutton's*.

For with its domed skylight, its chandeliers and its mirrors, Mutton's on the corner of West Street ('real turtle soup always available') was something of an institution. And towards its delights—'appetizing arrays of chickens, glazed tongues, meat pies, veal cakes and hams . . flanked by triumphs of fantastic confectionery'—Bede's heroine and her son were heading when they came across two pretty girls in front of the bookshop near St Paul's.

'Are you going to mattins?' the one was asking the other.

'No, I am going to Mutton's' laughed her companion, whose long brown hair was glistening after a bathe in the sea. 'Mutton's and Mattins. What a difference!'

'A difference indeed! And I think that it symbolises the two great classes into which Brighton society seems to be divided.'

'Ah! I see what you mean' responded the jolly one. 'Carnal and spiritual, isn't that it? And I fancy that the majority prefer Mutton's to Mattins.'

Plainly that was what they did. Indeed contemplating the throngs of fashionable folk strolling up and down the front, Richard Jefferies (that poetical mystic whose books are once more in vogue) felt bound to exclaim: 'It is a Piccadilly crowd by the sea—exactly the same style of people you meet in Piccadilly, but freer in dress and particularly in hats . . . These well-dressed and leading people never look at the sea. Watching by the gold-plate shop you will not observe a single glance in the direction of the sea, beautiful as it is, gleaming under the sunlight. They do not take the slightest interest in sea, or sun, or sky, or the fresh breeze calling white horses from the deep. Their pursuits are purely "social", and neither ladies nor gentlemen ever go on to the beach or lie where the surge comes to the feet. The beach is ignored; it is almost, perhaps quite vulgar . . . the sea is not "the thing" in Brighton.'

57. December 1882—a snowy scene outside the Old Ship

58. Watching the snowflakes fall from inside the comfort of Mutton's in 1882. Mutton's was a much celebrated place in the King's Road which combined the role of a confectioner's shop, hotel, dispenser of wines and spirits with several dining rooms. In 1876, J. Ashby-Sterry wrote:
Though folks may call me glutton
I do not care a button
But love a lunch with Mutton—
At this London-by-the-Sea.

59. *George Cruikshank's view of the Brighton scene in 1871*

A glance at Cuthbert Bede's own water colour dubbed *Brighton Beach 1864* will explain this reluctance. Hampstead Heath on a bank holiday was arcadian in comparison to the seaside once cheap day return tickets had been introduced.

It would be an overstatement to suggest that the barbarians were within the gates and the glory had fled—or was moving to Hove, where in contrast to the ebullience of Brighton, life was described as being 'tranquil and ornate' and the residents spent their days 'at golf, bicycling or At Homes'.

It would also be anachronistic; for Brunswick Square, Adelaide Crescent, and even the area of Cliftonville were still known as West Brighton in Victorian days. That is how the residents headed their notepaper. Behind

Adelaide Crescent there was a sheep farm with a gravel pit and a piggery. And stretching all the way towards the modest street called Hove Drove were market gardens. When the County Cricket ground was opened in 1871, its site was formerly a nine acre field of barley.

Back in 1830, Decimus Burton had planned a new estate for Isaac Lyon Goldsmid on a derelict brickyard just beyond Lansdowne Place. By royal permission, it was named after Queen Adelaide. But only ten houses were built before work on the project was stopped; Adelaide Crescent was not actually completed for another 30 years. However, this did not deter Goldsmid from financing a huge conservatory just behind his estate.

The Antheum (from the Greek anthos, meaning flower) was constructed entirely of cast-iron and glass. 164 feet in diameter and 64 feet high, it was to have been the largest structure of its kind in the world. The interior was laid out as an exotic garden, with gravel walks, rare tropical trees and flowering shrubs. There was even a small lake with fishes and aquatic plants. To support the enormous weight of the dome, the architect planned to have a central pillar with an observation gallery around it. But unfortunately the engineers decided to dispense with the pillar, with the result that an hour after the temporary supports were removed the girders buckled, and the whole structure came crashing to the ground. Twenty years went by before the tangled wreckage of twisted girders and broken glass was cleared

60. Some Brighton fishermen in a photograph of 1871. The fishermen were an independent breed as indeed they had to be. Not only did they have the uncertainty of the elements to contend with but also the actions of the authorities. For instance, the Steine which by tradition was their place for mending boats and drying nets, was put out of bounds to them and became a fashionable promenade instead. Then they had to share the beach with an increasing number of bathing machines and impatient visitors

61. *Cuthbert Bede painted this picture of Brighton Beach in 1864. Somewhat optimistically one feels, he depicts visitors, pie sellers, children, balloon hawkers, fishermen, boats and bathing machines co-existing happily*

62. *The newly opened Aquarium featured on the front page of* The Illustrated London News, *10 August 1872*

away to build Palmeira Square on the site of this ill-fated venture.

After Adelaide Crescent had finally been completed, the convergence westwards gathered momentum. During the 1860s, Cliftonville became fashionable. Unlike other developments, it grew up plot by plot, with no overall plan. The owners could build as they wished; in a single street were to be seen Tudor chimneys, Dutch gables, Regency replicas, and turretted mansions. This was followed in the 1870s by the meticulously planned West Brighton estate with its broad avenues of solid Victorian houses, which were given numbers instead of names, while the great sweep of Grand Avenue measured 70 feet across from kerb to kerb.

Such rapid growth from scratch in so very few years led people to say that Hove sprang into existence with the rapidity of a trans-Atlantic town.

Of course there were developments in the central parts of Brighton too. The great aquarium, sunk deeply into the ground like a Victorian cathedral that had been engulfed by the waves (or, if you prefer, a Pompeian court) was opened in 1872. Volk's Electric Railway—surely one of the first electric trains in the world—was built to run from a point just beyond the Palace Pier to Black Rock. And when the old Chain Pier was destroyed by a storm in 1896, it was replaced by the Palace Pier which, with its penny-in-the-slot machines that showed saucy pictures of 'What the Butler Saw' at the turn of a handle, and its gruesomely realistic animated models (tombs that gave up ghosts and skeletons, the condemned man on the guillotine), seemed somehow to have a naughtier, more raffish air about it than its counterpart along the front. Though it may have been less suitable for children, it was greater fun all the same. Finally the opening of the new Metropole Hotel—always regarded as the ugliest building in town and a magnet for the flashy 'fast set'—reinforced, in many people's minds, the contrast between the racy vulgarity of Brighton and the decorous atmosphere of Hove.

Prinked and select, Hove became a haven for professional people and retired Empire-builders who held themselves self-consciously aloof from

63. *The sea-lions were a great attraction at the Brighton Aquarium. They arrived in 1876 and the local newspaper was soon reporting that they 'appear to have fully overcome the ill effects of their trans-Atlantic voyage'. Amongst the interested visitors who came to see them in 1876 was Lewis Carroll who had also visited the Aquarium within days of its opening in 1872. This engraving appeared in* The Illustrated London News *on 6 January 1877*

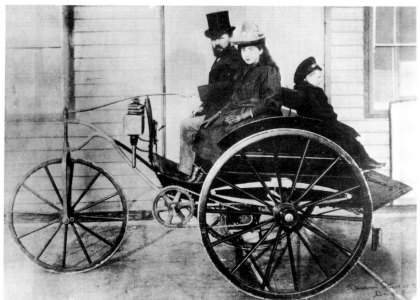

64. *This photograph of Magnus Volk in his electric dog-cart was taken in October 1887. Beside him is his 17-year-old sister-in-law Deborah, while his son Bert is seated behind. Underneath the seat was the boot which held the battery weighing 40 lbs. The dog-cart could be driven at either 3½ or 7 miles an hour*

the goings-on down town in Brighton (though they enjoyed its amenities). In Hove, the pace was slow. Conventions were upheld. It was considered quite the thing to dine at the Old Ship or give coming-out parties at the Grand, but socially demeaning to be seen at the Metropole.

'They were tremendous houses in Adelaide Crescent' recalls Margaret Powell, who went to work as a kitchen maid for the Rev. and Mrs Clydesdale around 1922. 'They started off with a basement and went up to an attic. There were 132 stairs in all, and the basements were dark like dungeons. The front of the basement, with iron bars all down the bay windows, was the servants' hall. When you were sitting there all you saw going by was people's legs. The light had to be on all day long.'

65. *Looking at this photograph it is not difficult to see why the Brighton and Rottingdean Seashore Electric Railway which opened in 1896 was nicknamed Daddy Longlegs. It was the invention of Magnus Volk (1851–1937) the Brighton pioneer of electrical engineering. Daddy Longlegs could travel through the waves on its 24-foot-long legs and electricity was conveyed by means of overhead wires. The railway, however, was too fragile to cope with the violence of winter seas and only lasted for five years*

66. *The saloon of the Daddy Longlegs was 12 feet wide and 25 feet long and was comfortably fitted out. Much of the space was occupied by a double ottoman and a novel idea was the potted plants and flowers which sprouted from the central space. There was a stained glass dome in the middle of the ceiling and plate glass windows all round*

67. *The Metropole was opened in 1890. It was designed by Alfred Waterhouse, the famous Victorian architect, who was also responsible for the Natural History Museum at South Kensington. The Metropole's impressive pile was rendered yet more aggressive because of its red brick and terracotta which was a stark contrast to the traditional cream stucco work of the Regency terraces. In view of its somewhat theatrical splendour, it is not surprising it was much frequented by people such as the Gaiety girls and their admirers*

Though the Crescent still looks much as it did 60 years or indeed a century ago, with gardens all down the centre, life has changed a good deal since then. In that spacious era, the milkman used to call three times a day; the butcher and the greengrocer came round for orders every morning. In the absence of refrigerators, food was conserved in a big galvanised metal box, and the ice-man brought a block of ice each morning as well. After breakfast, Mrs Clydesdale would interview the cook and give her the menus for the day.

The kitchen staff were kept busy. 'We used to get lovely bones from the butcher which cook would stew in a saucepan on the side of the range all day long with herbs in a little muslin bag, and with a carrot, onion, swede, or

68. *This painting of about 1880 captures the essence of the old and the new Brighton. In the foreground there is the traditional activity of boats and fishermen; while to the right rise the modern hotels—the Grand and the Metropole—and to the left a paddle steamer lies alongside the West Pier*

69. *In March 1883 hordes of soldiers descended on Brighton for the Volunteer Review. This entailed sham fights and manoeuvres on the Downs, church parades, of course, and a little relaxation with the fair sex. Newspaper artists were kept busy portraying the scenes and this charming study of a walk on the Chain Pier appeared in the* Pictorial World

turnip. In the evening she would take all these out and put in egg-shells (not the eggs themselves, just the shells) and vigorously whisk it. Every bit of scum then came to the top and was skimmed; greaseproof paper was laid on top to absorb the fat. Sometimes we laid a dozen pieces. The soup came out a pale golden colour, but as clear as water.'

Mayonnaise, hollandaise and horseradish sauces were all done by hand. Potatoes were cut into slices so thin that they were almost transparent. 'You laid each one separately on a cloth, then you covered them with another cloth until they dried. You melted a portion of lard in a very deep frying pan and dropped the crisps in one by one.'[4]

The man of God had his foibles too. He wore black boots all the week, but brown boots on Sundays. They had to be polished underneath and the bootlaces (which were half an inch wide) always had to be ironed. Though he had a car and a chauffeur of his own, this did not stop him from engaging a hackney carriage to call twice a week at the door, driven by an elderly man called Ambrose. Tradition obviously died hard.

Margaret remembers how up and down Adelaide Crescent were cars with smartly uniformed chauffeurs. They wore knee-breeches and shiny boots, peaked caps and white gloves. They stood rigidly to attention by the limousines and landaulettes, ready for the moment when their employers came out. Punctually on the stroke of ten, the Crescent sprang into action. 'It started at the house next door but one from ours. The door opened and out came an old gentleman. He was helped down the stairs by the butler. Then came the old lady on the arm of the housemaid, the under-housemaid

4. Once, when serving at table, there was an accident. 'I was so nervous my hand started shaking. The dish shot down the salver and all the potatoes shot over an attractive French woman. She jumped up and let out a stream of French words I couldn't understand. Then I saw that some of the potatoes had got lodged in her cleavage, so I tried to get them out with a serving spoon. The silly thing didn't keep still—they must have been burning her—anyway instead of getting them out I squashed them against her breast. She flung the spoon out of my hand and screamed "coshon" about half a dozen times.' Margaret fled. Only later did she find out that 'cochon' meant pig.

70. *Brighton sea-front viewed from one of the piers gains quite a different perspective. But not everyone wants a pier for a neighbour and the residents of Regency Square complained bitterly when the West Pier was built opposite to them. From this vantage point on the West Pier the scene is dominated by the Grand Hotel which was the largest and tallest hotel in the town when it was opened in 1864. It contained 300 rooms and a great innovation was the lift, called an ascending omnibus*

71. *A cartoon depicting a crowd of men at the entrance to the Old Ship in about 1890—note the absence of ladies—the downstairs Smoking Room had the aura of an exclusive gentlemen's club*

72. *This group of people (including a prettily clad baby with its basket-work pram) stands in Pool Valley. At one time it was liable to flooding either from the sea or from the intermittent stream called the Wellsbourne which flowed south from the Steine. In the background stands Cowley's Bunn Shoppe built in 1794 and faced with black mathematical tiles. Brill's Baths are on the corner to the left. In 1862 Charles Brill extended his premises to this site in Pool Valley with what was described as the only sea-water swimming baths for ladies in the whole of Europe. Queen Mary is said to have learnt swimming here*

carrying a footstool and a horrible old-looking lap dog. The pair was ushered into the car, the footstool was arranged under the old gentleman's feet, and the dog was tenderly placed on the old lady's lap. The chauffeur leaned in and carefully wrapped a rug around both of them, and off they

73. An advertisement of 1894

went. This scene was repeated all around the Crescent. These were the ten o'clock totterers.'

Which brings us to the next great stage in Brighton's development: the advent of the Car.

21. The Palace Pier at sunset

22. Motor Rally outside the Old Ship in 1908

23. Rex Whistler's painting *The Spirit of Brighton*

24. Rottingdean windmill

25. Modern-day beach scene

CHAPTER 12

Edwardian Glow

74. *A warm summer day on the sea-front opposite to the Old Ship in about 1902. The window blinds were fitted to the hotel in 1890 at a cost of £133 14s 9d*

A beau on a bike seems an unlikely conjunction. Yet back in the days of George IV, a primitive wooden device resembling a scooter with a saddle was all the rage among the dandies. With a little nifty footwork they could reach a speed of ten miles an hour on their 'dandy-horses'; in fact one of them made the trip to Brighton in under nine hours.

Forty years later the velocipede, which at least had pedals, grew into that iron monstrosity, the penny-farthing, with its dangerous propensity to tip over forwards at a touch of the brake. You had to be pretty keen to dress up in a brass-buttoned pea-jacket and a pill-box hat and wobble precariously along, as cycling clubs did, behind a bugler in full song. Sir Harry Preston, who later acquired the derelict Royal York Hotel and then the Royal Albion, tells us that he loved riding his penny-farthing. But he admits that the way he and his friends put up their legs and coasted down some of the hills outside Brighton made him wonder that any of them returned alive.

So it was just as well that a Brighton clockmaker named Harry Lawson devised his 'safety bicycle' with two equal sized wheels. When first put through its paces in a race from Brighton to Shoreham in 1876, Lawson's new machine was derided by the penny-farthing enthusiasts, who called its riders 'monkeys-on-a-stick'. But it was what the general public wanted. Soon the Brighton road was crowded with purposefully pedalling cyclists of both sexes.

Once the factories in Coventry started producing these safety bicycles by the thousand, cycling entered its golden age. Even so, people were already

75. The interior of the Old Ship's lounge in about 1904. Note the solid leather arm chairs and the more delicate wicker ones in the background

beginning to think what a blessing it would be if only the bicycle could propel them rather than the other way round. 'If I could build a little engine and use its power to do the propelling, and if I could use a regular carriage instead of a bicycle, there would be no limit to where I could go' mused Hiram Maxim in Massachusetts, unaware that two Germans were doing just that. Though Carl Benz and Gottlieb Daimler both set about adapting Otto's atmospheric engine for the motive power, they approached the problem in different ways. Whereas Benz sought to build a motor vehicle from scratch, Daimler fitted his engine into a carriage and dispensed with the horse.

If no one man actually invented the car, it arrived a hundred years ago in a world that needed it, but was hardly prepared for its advent. In Britain, still wedded to the horse, motoring was regarded more as a sport than a commercial proposition. Crippled as they were by the notorious Red Flag Act, British engineers continued to concentrate on producing cycles—to such good effect, what's more, that Coventry controlled the world's trade in bicycles and tricycles. Indeed it was into British tricycles that the continental innovators first fitted their motors.

Though Britain ruled the waves, the few cars to be found around the country were nearly all imported, and could only be driven freely in private grounds. True, Frederick Simms acquired Daimler's patent rights and formed the Daimler Motor Syndicate in 1893. And Henry Sturmey, then editor of *The Cyclist*, started a weekly motoring magazine which he called

the *Autocar*—his choice of a generic name to replace 'horseless carriage'. (As an ex-schoolmaster, he objected to the mixed use of Greek and Latin roots in 'automobile'.)

But thanks to Harry Lawson, Brighton can lay some claim to have acted as a catalyst, if that is an acceptable word in motoring circles. For fully a year before it became legal to drive a motor car at more than walking pace, the flamboyant Lawson, who by now had amassed a tidy fortune floating cycle concerns, conceived the grandiose scheme of cornering the whole of the nation's yet unborn motor industry. Launching the so-called British Motor Syndicate, he set about acquiring all existing and future patents, and in a sense to create an industry from scratch.

First, of course, it was necessary to overcome the opposition of numerous vested interests, for though many inventions have been greeted with suspicion, it is difficult to visualise the depth of hostility that the horseless carriage aroused. So, meeting at weekends in the downstairs bar at the Old Ship, Lawson and his friends formed themselves into a pressure group called the Motor Car Club that kept hammering away at the government with the message that the horseless carriage was not so antisocial as people seemed to think; that they were a persecuted minority, misunderstood and deprived of their rights. Finally this alliance between the cycle trade and a handful of enthusiastic aristocrats was eloquent enough to win Parliament around. In November 1896 the antiquated Locomotives Act was finally amended, and the speed limit fixed at 14 m.p.h., though local authorities were permitted to reduce this if necessary (which they promptly did—to 12 m.p.h.).

One can imagine the jubilation at the Old Ship bar. Glasses were raised, heads put together, and plans immediately devised to celebrate this lifting of the shackles. There would have to be an Emancipation Run. From

76. A motor rally outside the Old Ship in about 1908. In 1906 the hotel became the headquarters of the Automobile Club. The iron gas lamp standards were removed in 1909 after one had been damaged by a passing vehicle

77. *Sir Harry Preston took over the Royal York in 1901 and the Royal Albion in 1913. They were two of Brighton's historic hotels but at the time they were ailing and run down. He did so much more than just revitalise them. His enthusiasm for flying, boxing, motoring, yachting and the theatre was infectious and he was also a skilful promoter. He was largely responsible for the earliest motor racing events being held on Madeira Drive, and for the formation of the Sussex Motor Yacht Club*

London to Brighton—from one Metropole Hotel to the other!

On 14 November, the day that cars could at last move freely on British roads, they foregathered for breakfast at the appointed place. Ceremoniously the Earl of Winchelsea tore a red flag in two. Then at the helm of the Panhard which had won the Paris–Bordeaux race a year before, Harry Lawson led off a procession of some 30 solid-tyred, tiller-steered machines through the drizzle. The rain increased, the wind got up, and no two reports agree on the number of cars that took part, nor how many reached Brighton to be greeted by the Mayor under a banner flapping in the gale at Preston Park. It assured them, however, that 'Centuries will look upon this, your immortal ride.'

Regrettably it must be said that Lawson's tempting prospectuses resulted in several million pounds being invested in his syndicate, only to be quickly lost. When, shortly after the Brighton Run, it began to look as though investors might be on the receiving end of a sting, the Motor Club was quickly replaced by a genuine body set up to protect, encourage and develop motoring. The Automobile Club of Great Britain and Northern Ireland—later the RAC—was formally inaugurated on 10 August 1897. But by a collusion of timing, chemistry and happy economics, that most genial of characters, Harry Preston, kept Brighton at the centre of the motoring stage.

Preston it was who persuaded the Town Council, against considerable opposition, to lay a tarmac surface on Madeira Drive which could serve as a motor racing track. 'In the summer of 1905, I remember, we had a great fight, the sporting and enterprising element against the stick-in-the-mud element, to get a motor racing track—the first of its kind—laid down along the sea-front between the Palace Pier to within a quarter of a mile of Black Rock' he recalls in his memoirs. 'I had been asked by the secretary of the Royal Automobile Club, Julian Orde, if I could arrange for a race to take place under the Club's auspices.' The Mayor, Mr Fred Blaker, was enthusiastic, so he arranged a little lunch to discuss the affair, for the Club insisted on a tarmac track. 'The stick-in-the-muds on the Town Council were absolutely opposed to anything so revolutionary, but the progressives won the day; the famous tarmac road was specially laid, and down came all the boys—and girls too—with a wierd and wonderful collection of machines . . . The Madeira Terrace, the elevated walk running along the western seafront, was the "grand stand". Thousands of people watched the races (and the various collisions) from here, and all Brighton and half England talked of nothing else during those three exciting days.'

No wonder they did, for this was the first real competition to take place on British soil, where motor racing had hitherto been prohibited (the Gordon Bennett Cup had to be run in Ireland) and many of the drivers who took part are famous in the annals of motoring. One thinks of the Hon C. S. Rolls, Clifford Earp, S. F. Edge, Charles Jarrott, Lord Brabazon of Tara, Sir Ralph Gore, K. L. Guinness, and Theodore Schneider, founder of the Schneider Air Trophy.

Strolling along the front from the Old Ship, people caught their first sight of the huge 'dust and glory' machines that had taken part in the legendary city-to-city races on the continent, and (says the *Gazette*) some were frightened to go near them as they throbbed with a noise like a terrific

Brighton, Madeira Road,
"Our Morning Ride."

cannonading, belching petrol fumes and seemed apparently on the point of bursting into fragments. But it was refreshing to see Mr Schneider start. 'No oil-stained, dirty grimed overall for him. A dapper, pleasant figure in blue serge, with a white carnation in his button-hole, a cigarette between his lips on the famous rush along the Madeira Drive, with none of the worried anxious looks which the other competitors wear.'

The meeting was, in fact, rather an elegant affair. On Ladies' Day the men turned out in frock coats with Panama hats, and the ladies' dresses were a riot of colour: light tailor-made costumes and blouses in every shade of silk, with immense parasols. Mrs Bennett-Stanford from Preston Manor took to the wheel wearing a muslin dress with blue spots and a large biscuit coloured hat secured by a veil. However, Mrs Herbert Lloyd, more practically attired in a light dust coat and goggles, put up the fastest time.

The Autocar Challenge Cup was won by S. F. Edge in Clifford Earp's 90 h.p. Napier at the astonishing speed of 97.2 m.p.h. (which was not far off the existing land speed record of 104.65) ahead of Brabazon's Mors, Gore's Mercedes, Guinness's Darracq, and Schneider's Rochet-Schneider. Not bad, when you think of it. Cars were running away from the past into the future.

Just two months later, in fact, the first motor bus service started up between London and Brighton. The double-decked Vanguard did the trip in 4½ hours, and soon charabancs were trundling regularly down the Brighton road. 'King Petrol, with a rush and a roar, is advancing on his all-conquering career' exulted a Brighton magazine. 'It is King Petrol who will help his Bride-by-the-sea to retain her supremacy.'

Prophetic words! Yet even as motor transport began changing the

78. A charming postcard of two children in one of the popular goat-carts. The little girl is delighted to be photographed but her companion is not so sure about it. In the background can be seen the iron trellis-work of the Madeira Terrace which was opened on 24 May 1890. It took seven years to build and 600 tons of iron were used. At the centre of each arch was the head of a Neptune alternating with that of an Aphrodite

79. A charabanc outing of the
1920s pictured at Madeira Drive.
It was just as well that hats were de
rigueur, because a trip in this old
boneshaker of 28 seats was
draughty to say the least

morphology of Britain, there were other excitements in store. Soon after his
arrival in Brighton, Harry Preston gave up sailing for motor yachting and
acquired *My Lady Ada*, the first and only motor-cruiser on this stretch of
the coast. When a torpedo boat flotilla came up on a visit from Portsmouth,
she became Brighton's first official flagship, chugging along with the
Mayor and Corporation on board. The visitors were given breakfast at
8.30 a.m.—hock with the fish, Pommery with the kidneys and bacon,
and liqueurs with the toast and marmalade—after which the Sussex
Motor Yacht Club was formed, and motor boat races added to the town's
attractions.

From motoring to flying was not a long call. Around the same time
André Beaumont, the French pioneer aviator, brought his Blériot mono-
plane over in pieces from Dieppe and assembled it on the beach at Black
Rock. 'You never saw such a box of tricks,' recalls Harry Preston, who
agreed to go up with him. 'It looked as if he had knocked it up out of soap
boxes and piano wire. When I took my seat beside him in the flimsy thing,
and the engine started with a rattle and a bang, the whole queer contraption
quivered as if it were going to fall to bits.' As they skimmed over the water,
rocking and shaking, he thanked his stars he was a good swimmer. But
suddenly the water ceased to rush past in a great wave on either side. The
craft skimmed and rose. 'We were in the air—we were flying. I saw the
green tumbled waters receding below. Beaumont swung her round and
mounted higher. We were in the air for three-quarters of an hour, and then
we landed with a splash.'

Flying in its infancy provided thrills not to be experienced today. Claude
Grahame-White once took Preston up for a joy-ride. 'He wanted to show

me the Royal Albion from the air, and he came in so low that I thought he was going to hit the chimneys. Just then George Graves looked out of a window and waved a handkerchief. Grahame-White turned to smile at me—and we just missed the telegraph wires by inches.'

It was Oscar Morrison, however, who flew the first plane into Brighton. Piloting another Blériot he came over from Brooklands aerodrome, taking 65 minutes to do the 40 miles. Afterwards he said he would have made better time had he not mistaken Worthing for Brighton—until, leaning over the side to get a better look, he spotted that there was only one pier, whereas Brighton had two. So banking round over gaping faces in the Sussex fields, he headed along the coast until the twin piers appeared, and landed on the beach between them. Not surprisingly, he broke his propeller on the pebbles.

Of course he was the hero of the hour, for aviation history was made on that February afternoon in 1911. Lots of people became bitten with the flying craze, and John Bacon still has in his possession a Christmas card depicting a party of guests arriving at the hotel in a balloon.

All this was emblematic of the Edwardian years, so full of confidence and well-heeled bravura. Yet only a little while earlier, during the last years of Queen Victoria's reign, Brighton had passed through a period of decadence, becoming, in the words of Lewis Melville, a 'Cockney's paradise, the Mecca of the stockbroker and the chorus-girl.' Its glory, grumbled Melville, had departed. The Pavilion was now an object of derision; the Steine was encircled by a network of tramways. Though Brighton might boast mammoth hotels, theatres and music-halls, the town offered everything but quiet.

Perhaps Melville had a point. The huge Metropole Hotel was certainly a monument to vulgarity and on the Promenade in front of it a concert party who called themselves 'The White Coons' gave performances, decked out in white suits, white Homburg hats, and stiff double collars. At the Hippodrome, Fred Karno presented his 'Screaming Sketch' called 'Saturday to Monday' (in which, playing a small part, was a young comedian named Charlie Chaplin). The most popular venue in town was now the variety show at the Grand Theatre, largely because smoking was permitted. Paddle steamers, such as the famous *Brighton Belle*, offered pleasure trips along the coast, there were donkeys for children on the beach and, had you looked out of the windows of the Old Ship, you would have seen minstrels with blackened faces playing banjos on the lower promenade outside.

Whereas Brighton had once been the 'Queen of the South', one of its aldermen was seriously advocating turning the resort into a Blackpool show-fair, with swings and roundabouts, an Eiffel tower and the hockey-pockey man. And it looked as if the alderman was getting his way.

Full board at the Old Ship (like the Grand) was now as little as 10s 6d a day. When Robert Bacon died in November 1888, his son Gresham became the owner. On the advice of his brother-in-law, the solicitor Harry Warne, the hotel was turned into a limited liability company and a manager put in to run it. If Gresham gradually turned his attention to other affairs, it may have been an indication that he shared these pessimistic views. Harry Preston himself admits that the Royal York was derelict when he took it over, 'like one of those decrepit noblemen whose line has gone to

80. *The Old Ship decorated for Edward VII's coronation*

seed', and as late as 1906 the *Daily Mail* ran a front page story condemning Brighton as an unattractive and outdated holiday resort. (Though when Preston indignantly rushed up to London and gave the editor a piece of his mind, the newspaper sportingly retracted and printed a more favourable description the following day.)

Fortunately the car and the King came to breathe new life into the town. As Prince of Wales, he had occasionally been down for some ceremony or other, but in the last years of his life Edward VII often stayed with his daughter, the Duchess of Fife, at No 1 Lewes Crescent. He was also fond of visiting his friend Arthur Sassoon, who lived in great style at 8 King's Gardens, Hove, attended by a legion of servants.[1]

So, once again Brighton was the haunt of a prince who loved good living and pretty women. There was nothing formal about his visits. Anyone who wished could see King Edward VII strolling in the gardens of Lewes Crescent or sitting in one of the sun shelters on the front at Hove, both of which areas were renamed in his honour: the eastern end of the Marine Parade became King's Cliff, and the Hove front Kingsway. Admiring subjects would sniff the aroma of his Havana as he walked arm-in-arm with his host, and confectioners displayed letters of commendation from Mrs Sassoon indicating how much his Majesty had enjoyed their cakes. 'The King is declared to be deriving both health and enjoyment from his holiday' observed the *Herald* in 1908, 'and the fact that he has been rejoicing in floods of sunshine is being chronicled in the press the country over.

1. Originally from Baghdad, the Sassoon family had grown into powerful merchants in India and China before retiring to become the Rothschilds of Brighton: Henry Labouchère used to joke that Brighton was a 'sea-coast town, three miles long and three yards wide, with a Sassoon at each end and one in the middle.'

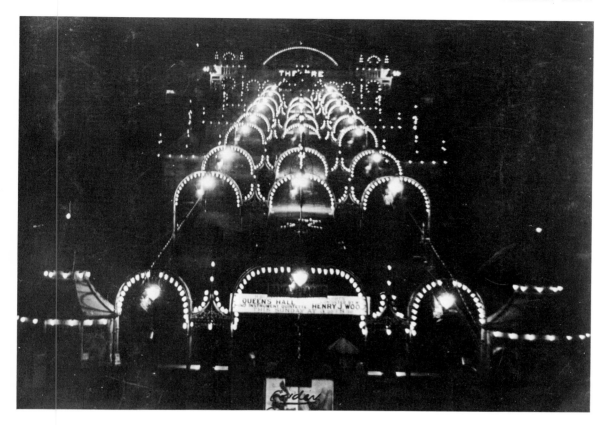

Nothing could exert a finer influence on the fortunes of Brighton.'

Which was certainly true. The monarch's presence brought back many of the fashionable visitors who had deserted the town, encouraging the railways to start running a luxury train, the *Southern Belle*, which did the trip from London in one hour. And for those with a hankering for nostalgia, A. G. Vanderbilt laid on a coach drawn by five American horses which drew up every evening at the door of the Old Ship.

Now Walter Winans, the American millionaire and champion driver of trotting horses, could be seen flashing along the sea-front in his rubber-tyred carriage amid the Daimlers and Silver Ghosts. At the Royal York, Arnold Bennett was busy writing *Clayhanger* and its sequel *Hilda Lessways*, both of which contained some graphic descriptions of Brighton in these Edwardian days. Later, in *Three Houses*, Angela Thirkell was to recall the summers she spent at Rottingdean with her grandparents, Sir Edward Burne-Jones, the Pre-Raphaelite painter, and Lady Burne-Jones, who was Rudyard Kipling's aunt, while Kipling wrote his *Just So Stories* in a nearby house. (They were a poor thing in print compared with the fun of hearing them told in 'cousin Ruddy's deep unhesitating voice', she thought. 'There was an inimitable cadence, an emphasis of certain phrases, a hint of intoning here and there which made his telling unforgettable.')

In those days Walter Sickert, who had a studio in Sussex Place, headed what came to be known as the Camden Town group of painters, which included the impressionist Robert Bevan. Bevan lived at Hove, not far from

81. The Palace Pier by night in about 1909. The name of the famous conductor Mr Henry Wood (knighted in 1911) appears on the billboard over the entrance. Although he earned an international reputation as a conductor of the Queen's Hall symphony and promenade concerts, he enjoyed touring the provinces too

82. A nostalgic glimpse of the Brighton Queen—once one of the most popular excursion steamers in the whole of the British Isles. She was built in 1897 at Glasgow and was famous for being a good timekeeper. She was taken over by the Admiralty during the First World War and was sunk in 1915. Curiously enough the second Brighton Queen (re-named thus in 1933) had a similar demise in 1940. A popular excursion steamer, she joined the many small boats which answered the call to help evacuate the British soldiers stranded at Dunkirk and was sunk there

83. The 'Tantivy' (pictured here in 1913) was one of the coaches which used to call at the Old Ship. Another was the 'Old Berkeley'—later owned by Bertram Mills. Both the 'Tantivy' and the 'Old Berkeley' are now to be found in the USA

George Albert Smith, the inventor of Kinemacolor, who was by this time exporting as many as 400 copies of his films a week to the United States—mostly small comic episodes that lasted for a minute or two.

Big names were back at the Theatre Royal. Paderewski, Melba, Clara Butt, Backhouse and Misha Elman performed at the Dome. A pilot looped the loop over Shoreham; a race took place between the first hydroplane and Harry Preston's motor yacht. W. G. Grace made 217 not out at Brighton—and was then bowled out first ball by a local bricklayer at a house-party match the following week. And Johnnie Douglas, having been called LBW at Hove, initiated the twentieth-century tradition of abusing the umpire. ('Where's your dog?' he asked him. 'What d'you mean?' 'Well you're the first —— blind man I've seen without his —— dog.')

The Sussex Racing Fortnight at Goodwood, Plumpton, Lewes and Brighton attracted more visitors than ever, now that so many of them could drive down by car. But some stockbrokers came on foot. Of the 87 competitors who took part in the Brighton Stock Exchange Walk, 77 finished—including Andrew Pringle, who covered the whole distance in topper and tailcoat. The winner, a Mr Broad, made it in $9\frac{1}{2}$ hours, and a rumour that eight stockbrokers had died on the way was scotched when the victims were discovered boisterously popping champagne corks in the Old Ship bar, having completed the last few miles by train.

Yes, the fizz and the sparkle had returned to Brighton. And never more so than in the summer of 1914, when newspapers exulted over the town's mounting prosperity as the crowds poured in for that fateful August Bank holiday. So packed were the trains that people stood all the way in the guards' vans. Since April there had been nothing but sunshine, and if the glorious weather continued it would be a brilliant year . . .

CHAPTER 13

Between the Wars

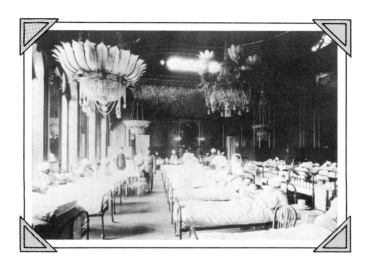

Though the Great War could have broken out at any time during the past ten years, when it finally came the day after August Bank Holiday in 1914, the nation was taken by surprise. People felt that if the Balkan states chose to cut each others' throats, that was only to be expected; but it was ridiculous to think that the two Triple Alliances would start a wholesale European war. The *Gazette* considered that there was 'little sign of the war cloud' that week-end.

Three days later the newspaper had changed its tune. 'Long anticipated by a few, and persistently scouted by many, the great conflagration of Europe has broken out' it stated. 'The time has come for the test. Every Englishman and woman must do their duty.' It added that Brighton had resolved to 'keep on smiling'.

That last remark just about summed up the local scene during the next four years. Reporting on 22 August that Brussels had fallen, the newspaper was consoled to see that 'Brighton is itself again'. The hotels were full once more, the shops were busy; traffic on the railways, trams and buses was normal, and the shock of the previous fortnight had vanished.

True, the town was soon invaded by hundreds of French and Belgian refugees who had lost their homes in the German advance. Comparisons were made with Napoleon's threat to the Sussex coast just over a hundred years earlier. But if a few timid ladies bolted their doors in the belief that the Germans had already landed, the Southdown Hunt resolved to go on hunting in the normal way. They shared the general attitude of business as usual.

84. For two years, from 1914 until 1916, the Royal Pavilion together with the Dome and other buildings became the Indian Military Hospital. As many as 724 beds were crammed in but then not many hospital wards could boast such ornate lighting arrangements. Catering was a nightmare—no beef (because of the Hindus), no pork or bacon (because of the Moslems) and different kitchens and separate taps for drinking water had to be provided

85. A royal visit to the Indian
Military Hospital at Brighton.
King George V has his back to the
camera and he is with Queen Mary
and their only daughter Princess
Mary

86. This evocative scene of a bygone
summer was sent as a postcard in
1916. The Dome can be seen in the
background. It was erected for the
comfort of the royal horses by the
Prince Regent and it was
undoubtedly the most magnificent
set of stables to be found in Europe.
Today, the building serves as a
concert hall and, before the
Brighton Centre was built, it was
often used for conferences

THE DOME, BRIGHTON.

By the end of the year 'letters from the Front' together with lengthening
lists of casualties began appearing in the newspapers alongside the equally
long lists of hotel visitors. At the suggestion of King George V, the Royal
Pavilion was converted into a hospital for wounded Indian soldiers (some of
whom, recovering consciousness in those fantastic oriental surroundings,

87. The West Pier (with flags flying) on a warm summer's day in the 1920s. The small hooded vehicle parked in front of the motor car is an invalid carriage. There were plenty of these for hire along the seafront

Promenade and Bandstand, looking Towards Hove – Brighton

88. A view of the promenade, including the bandstand, looking west. The angel of peace statue in the distance was erected on the boundary of Brighton and Hove

imagined that they had died and were waking in paradise). Many of the larger houses were also converted into hospitals, and the town became crowded with convalescent ranks in shapeless blue flannel uniforms.

The news of the first Zeppelin raid on London in May 1915 brought more people flocking to this safer haven. There was an 'unexpected concentration of Society upon Brighton' observed the *Gazette*. Brighton also became a favourite place for members of the wartime coalition government to spend their week-ends. Lloyd George, Asquith or Horatio Bottomley, in company with members of the British and European aristocracy, were to be seen dining at adjoining tables in the Old Ship with financiers, actresses and war profiteers. Not surprisingly, some ordinary folk were inclined to ask 'is there a war on?' In fact, observes Musgrave, 'The name of Brighton became something of a byword in the popular press as a resort especially frequented by profiteers, munitions-millionaires and other vulgar nouveaux-riches, who rubbed shoulders with the aristocracy in the grand hotels of the town.'

89. This scene has a certain
American look about it but in fact it
was taken inside the Dome at one of
Harry Preston's annual boxing
tournaments which he organised to
raise money for charity. For
instance, in 1926 one of these
occasions raised £3,500 for local
hospitals. Famous boxers such as
Jack Dempsey and Bombardier
Billy Wells took part. In this
photograph Harry Preston is sitting
in the front row while on his right is
the Prince of Wales (later the Duke
of Windsor) and on his left is
Prince George, Duke of Kent

90. This photograph was taken on
a sunny day in 1927. West Street
is on the left and to the right a line
of bathing machines are still in use.
The different level of the King's
Road and the beach is evident and it
is interesting to reflect that this was
once the central part of the old town
of Brighthelmstone before the old
houses below the cliffs were swept
away by the sea

26. Marina

27. Lanes

28. Horse Driving Trials, Stanmer Park, 1984

29. The bombed Grand Hotel, October 1984

91. *It was a bright sunny day in November 1934 when this photograph was taken during an Anglers' Festival on the Palace Pier. As well as being an evocative picture of the calm before the storm, it also gives us a close-up of the splendid iron-work. During the Second World War, a section was removed from the middle of the pier to prevent it from being used as a landing stage by the enemy*

92. *A view of East Street festooned with decorations to celebrate the Silver Jubilee of King George V and Queen Mary in May 1935. This was not the only Brighton street to be decorated by any means—in fact up and down the country there was a wave of enthusiasm. The King was surprised and wrote 'I'd no idea they felt like that about me'*

145

93. There cannot be many places which can throw a municipal garden party with such an exotic backdrop. This garden party was held in June 1935

For the Old Ship this was nothing new. The hotel had lived through such moments before, and during these war years, along with the Royal Albion, it became a favourite venue for young officers back on leave from the front. But after the war Brighton's phenomenal prosperity diminished as the big spenders returned home, and the hectic wartime gaiety gave way to the sophisticated disenchantment of the Twenties.

Though the Bright Young Things dashed down in their 3 litre Bentleys and boat-tailed Hispano Suizas, to them Brighton seemed provincial, and Hove stodgy, compared with the brittle bubble and dazzle of Mayfair.

True there were moments that would have brought a gleam to the eye of Michael Arlen or indeed Noel Coward. I do not know in which hotel it happened, but a guest who had been celebrating was shown up to his room, or at least what the porter thought was his room. And carefully laid out on the bed was a dainty, lacy nightdress. The man took out his monocle and surveyed it solemnly.

'What's this?' he asked.

'That,' replied the porter, who was not sure whether the gentleman was expecting a lady or not, 'is a lady's night-dress, Sir.'

The man leant over and put his nose to its scented folds. Then he turned to the porter. 'Take it away,' he commanded, 'and fill it.'

Writers in residence—if only temporary—included Hilaire Belloc, J. C. Squire, G. K. Chesterton and Maurice Baring, who celebrated his fiftieth birthday with a dinner for some 30 friends. There were oysters and steak-and-kidney pudding, apple dumplings and Welsh Rarebit. Each guest had to compose a poem and make a speech. Belloc sang a chansonette, Squire trolled a roundelay, but Chesterton declared that his speech was illegible and his handwriting inaudible. At the liqueur stage, watched with great interest by them all, Maurice Baring did his trick with a champagne bottle. First he balanced it on his head, and then he delicately placed a glass of old brandy on top of the bottle of champagne. When this was successfully accomplished, and the contents consumed, he then crossed the road and baptised himself in the sea, clad in tails and topper. 'It is a rite,' he explained.

The Prince of Wales, then acclaimed as the world's most eligible bachelor, used to slip away from his official duties (and sentimental attachments with the witty Frieda Ward, or 'Toodles', the beautiful Thelma Furness) for a quiet day by the sea at Brighton. Usually he stayed with Sir Sydney Greville, Groom in Waiting to his father George V, who had a house in Hove. Sometimes, after dinner, the royal party would crowd into a small open car and drive down to see the Palace Pier Follies. On one occasion they walked unrecognised to the end of the pier, paid for their seats, and entered the crowded theatre just before the show ended.

'Do you think they would sing some more songs?' asked the Prince when the curtain went down. And sure enough the performance was repeated until he sent word that they must all be tired. After God Save the King was played for the second time, the crowd surged round him. The Prince had to shove his way through the jam to reach the stage, where he shook hands with every one of the performers. Human touches like this were what made him so popular in the Twenties.

All the same, social rumblings were to be heard. Indeed discontent among working men, exacerbated perhaps by the communists' seizure of power in Russia, led to the General Strike in 1926. In Brighton there was a particularly strong feeling of industrial unrest, due to the hundreds of railway workers employed in the area. So when residents awoke on the morning of 1 May, it was to find themselves in a 'strange and perplexing world' with all services at a standstill.

So accustomed are we now to trades' union strategies, that it is difficult to imagine the intense hatred that the strikers aroused in those days. One woman drove her two-seater car slap into a column of strikers that was converging on the Town Hall behind a blaring brass band. Many of the men had to jump for their lives, and the band's instruments flew off in every direction. With equal determination a large number of ordinary citizens responded to the government's appeal to keep public transport on the road. A corps of auxiliaries known as the 'mounted specials' was formed to protect these public-spirited volunteers (or 'blacklegs' in today's idiom; it depends on your sympathies) and on one occasion an ugly scuffle took place between them and a crowd of pickets guarding the entrance to the tramway depot. Bricks were hurled at the police; there were injuries on both sides; a quantity of arrests were made.

'The flying stones, the panic rush, the thud of blows, the shrieks of frightened women and children caught in the confusion invariably aroused by violence—these things do not belong in civilized Brighton', admonished the *Herald*. But unfortunately violence did not disappear from the scene once the General Strike ended. Around this time Brighton began to gain a vicious reputation from the gangs who infested the race-course, offering 'protection' to bookmakers and slashing their victims with razors in the poorer areas of the town. Graham Greene caught the sense of menace that these young toughs generated in his novel *Brighton Rock*, and a succession of killings, culminating in two notorious 'trunk murders' caused the town to be dubbed as 'The Queen of Slaughtering Places' by the more sensational press.

This was neither kind nor fair, since these sordid undercurrents were restricted to the slum area around Carlton Hill, which was demolished in the Thirties. But it reminds us that despite the Town Council's efforts to tackle social problems, there was still a good deal of real poverty in Brighton.

Margaret Powell makes the point poignantly, but with humour. 'I used to wonder why, when things were so hard, mum kept on having babies' she relates. But she soon found out. 'You see, it was the only pleasure poor people could afford. It cost nothing, at least at the time you were actually making the children. Later on, well, the working class people never looked ahead in those days. They didn't dare.

'Sunday afternoons were devoted to love-making, because there was not much privacy in working class families. When you lived in two or three rooms you had to have the children in the same room as you. So you see it was only when the children were out of the way that they could really let themselves go. That's why Sunday schools were so popular . . .'

If the phrase 'a land fit for heroes' was on everyone's lips, unfortunately it had a hollow ring. Yet Brighton was one of the few places which gave some reality to the sentiment by providing ex-servicemen with strips of land, enough for a small house and a vegetable garden. These can still be seen today up the London Road. And after the war, social improvements were continuously brought about, largely through the initiative of Sir Herbert Carden, a well-known solicitor who served for many years as alderman and mayor.[1] Indeed the Brighton Corporation pioneered several forms of civic enterprise, such as telephones, electricity and trams. It purchased downland to give the town a 'green belt', and constructed housing estates that received international acclaim.

In 1922, for instance, the Corporation built 500 new houses. And by then, even the poorest people could enjoy a taste of Brighton's gleaming prosperity. It was appropriate that the town which had fostered such innovative motion picture developments should also have had one of the very first super film 'palaces' to be built in Britain. When the Regent

1. Between 1928 and 1942 Stanley Theobald, who served on the local Councils for some 28 years, implemented Carden's policy of land buying for the Brighton Corporation. Amongst the more memorable purchases were all the properties north of the Western Road, which had to be bought for road widening schemes. (At one point the road was so narrow that two double-deckers could not pass each other.) The sites were then rented out, and even today prime locations such as that occupied by Marks & Spencer are owned by the Corporation.

Theobald likes to tell the story of how he bought Brighton Town Hall for £2,000. What he means, of course, is a pub called the Town Hall in Edward Street on the corner of Mount Pleasant.

Cinema opened in Queen's Road it was hailed as a 'gorgeous Temple of the Silent Drama'. In addition to accommodating 3,000 spectators it contained a huge foyer, restaurant and coffee-house; very probably it was indeed 'the largest, finest, most artistic kinematograph establishment in the country, if not in the world'.

Nine years later a second giant picture palace, the Savoy, this time with a Chinese interior, was erected on the site of Brill's Baths along the front from the Old Ship. And a little way off in the other direction, the great ferro-concrete mass known as S.S. Brighton was built to house the largest covered sea-water swimming pool in existence. But although a great many swimming championships were held there, the craze for skating must obviously have been stronger than that of indoor bathing, because in 1936 it was converted into one of the first artificial ice-rinks, and became the home of the celebrated Brighton Tigers.

I remember how eagerly we used to hurry along Western Road and then down West Street to reach the huge rink in time for the dancing session at eleven o'clock, when for a shilling a go you could waltz or tango with one of the glamorous (and oh, so patient) instructresses. In the centre of the ice, aspiring tyros traced their intricate figures—my cousin Vivienne won her silver medal on that rink—but the rest of us never seemed to tire of swooping endlessly around in what we fondly hoped was speed-skating style. In the evening, of course, the Tigers took over. At the time, they were one of the fastest teams on earth. There was also an ice show called *Marina*, as well as a succession of ballets, carnivals and pantomimes, all on ice.

Sherry's, right opposite, was out of bounds for my cousins and myself. It was thought rather raffish, and however excellent the food, the dancing and floor shows were déclassé in avuncular eyes. Brighton as a whole was discouraged after dark—for did not the Vicar of Hove consider that people there 'dabbled in excitements and revelled in sex'? But we were often taken to dances at the Grand and dinners at the Old Ship.

Part of the Regency-style façade of the Old Ship was rebuilt in 1935, incorporating some shops on the sea-front into a new dining room. Stuccoed white in those days, it neither attempted nor pretended to be a fashionable place, but retained the atmosphere of a large country house married to the intimacy of an old country inn. As my uncle would say, simple but perfectly cooked food and a cellar with a history going back to the old smuggling days went hand in hand with well-bred comfort and friendly service. For a lad like myself, largely brought up in the glittering ambience of Alexandria and Geneva, it seemed the epitome of Englishness. It was exciting to find Rafael Sabatini, the novelist, and his sculptress wife, who knew my parents in Switzerland, dining at a nearby table with James Agate, the critic, the lovely Frances Day, and David Murray, who was then editor of the *Times Literary Supplement*. Rumour had it that Tallulah Bankhead was also around, but I didn't meet her until much later in New York.

The Old Ship Garage, on the site of Saunder's cottages in Black Lion Street, was also rebuilt (in 1928) to provide accommodation for 120 cars—the most spacious hotel garage in the county. There was also a special annex, where bed, bath and breakfast for chauffeurs and personal valets cost 5s a night, or 10s for full board.

In the hotel itself, the charges for guests varied from 10s for a single room on the fifth floor to 35s for the best double rooms with private bath, including breakfast, of course. Inclusive terms, for a minimum of three days, ran from 16s 6d to 50s a day, and included afternoon tea and coffee after dinner. Luncheon, served in the Coffee-Room from one to three o'clock, cost 4s, and dinner, which was served from seven o'clock onwards, came to 6s, with an extra charge of 6d if brought up to one's private sitting room. These charges, which were in line with other hotels of a similar category (and comparable with big establishments in Switzerland and even Shepheard's in Cairo or Raffles in Singapore) must now be multiplied by about a factor of 30 to reach today's costs, which is a good indication of the inflation we have suffered over the last 50 years.

Five hundred pounds a year then had the purchasing power of £15,000 today, and many ordinary folk earned up to five times that amount. So there was more prosperity in the Thirties than social historians are often inclined to believe. With ten pounds a week you could run a small car and come down to Brighton; with £2,000 a year you were relatively well off. It depended, of course, on family commitments. Granted there was still a good deal of poverty, unemployment and social inequality in the country. Too many people still had to make do with squalid slum dwellings. The progress of social reform was far too slow. Even so, let's make no mistake about it: the majority of English men and women were contented enough with their lot as the war clouds began to gather in 1938. Though they hated dictatorships and looked on the rise of both Nazis and Fascists with dismay, they had no wish to get embroiled in another European conflict. They just wanted to get on with their lives.

The yo-yo craze symbolised the nation's feelings of hope and despair as the Prime Minister shuttled between London and Berchtesgaden. 'If you don't at first succeed, fly fly again' quipped E. R. G. Heath of Balliol at the Oxford Union. But the general mood was hardly one of epigrammatic cynicism. Indeed there was a sensation of almost animal relief when Chamberlain waved his piece of paper at the airport. All over the country people burst into tears and cried for joy that it was to be peace and not war.

Alas, barely a year later, World War II began.

CHAPTER 14
Fireworks and After

The Bore War, they called it at first, the Sitzkrieg. Despite the blackout, rationing, Home Guard duties, not to mention some 30,000 tearful children who were evacuated to Brighton and Hove in anticipation of intense air raids on London, there was a sense of anti-climax. Even a full meeting of the Allied Supreme War Council, with the British and French prime ministers and all the service chiefs in Hove Town Hall, did little to dispel the feeling that not much was happening. People sang songs like 'We're gonna hang out the washing on the Siegfried Line', and made jokes about unused air raid shelters or sandbagged statues. As they waited to be called up, their attitude once again was 'business as usual'.

Nine months went by before the illusion was shattered. At Brighton the first hint of disaster came one May morning when a seaplane made a forced landing among the holiday makers on the beach. From the windows of the Old Ship just opposite, bathers were seen helping jittery passengers out of the badly shot-up aircraft. Word soon got around that these were Dutch cabinet ministers. And not long afterwards, a party of diamond merchants arrived from Amsterdam with their bags full of industrial diamonds.

The Nazi invasion of Holland had begun. Upon which, as if to mock that flamboyantly beautiful spring, a flood of sinister tidings followed. Within less than a fortnight, the Low Countries were overrun and the Maginot Line pierced. Hemmed in and cut off from any possible retreat by land, the British Expeditionary Force had to be evacuated from Dunkirk.

In that epic operation, a number of vessels from Brighton took part.

94. *Standing under the guy-ropes of the Big Top, this enchanting group of girls worked for Bertram Mills' circus which visited Brighton in August 1939. The photograph was taken a few days before the outbreak of war and one cannot help wondering how it affected them*

95. *This is how the Old Ship looked in 1939. The old property on the corner of Black Lion Street was later demolished and the new wing constructed during 1963–4*

Many of them were lost. Mercilessly bombed as it carried 300 French soldiers to safety, the *Brighton Belle* went down, along with the *Brighton Queen* and two of the *Skylarks*. Fishing boats with names like *Our Doris* and *Cornsack* were sunk as they ferried to and fro from the bomb-blasted beaches.

More than 350,000 troops were saved: a staggering achievement. But when France surrendered on 17 June, and Churchill gravely told the Commons that 'the whole fury and might of the enemy must soon be turned against us', it became clear that Brighton was now at the sharp edge of the conflict.

So the beaches were mined. Army sappers blew holes in the middle of the piers. The seafront was barricaded with sandbags and barbed wire. Machine guns were set up at strategic points, and a battery of six-inch guns was sited on the front below Lewes Crescent. Yet when King George VI and Winston Churchill inspected these defences in the first days of July, they could not fail to be struck by the pathetic inadequacy of such protection against an enemy that had already blitzed its way across the continent. It was probable that Hitler had already issued orders for an invasion. Anyone who listened to Berlin radio could hear 'Lord Haw-Haw' boasting that the Führer intended to use the Royal Pavilion as his personal headquarters. Even if such bombastic statements were greeted with derision, nothing could alter the fact that Brighton was likely to be devastated should the Germans attempt to land. For all the national determination to repel any attack, it was hardly a comforting prospect.

Later, when the German documents came to light, it was found out that Hitler had taken the decision to invade Britain at the precise moment that Churchill was lunching at the Royal Albion on 2 July.[1] What's more, that

1. 'Looking out of the window,' Churchill recalled when receiving the Freedom of the Borough in 1947, 'I saw where the old Chain Pier used to stand, and saw the Grenadier Guards sandbagging the kiosks to repel a landing. One of the kiosks I had always known in my young days as being devoted to the performing flea. The particular performing flea we were concerned with at that time is not now performing, and for that fact we are entitled to rejoice in a great deliverance.'

the Fuehrer's initial directive called for an amphibious assault on the Brighton beaches, combined with a mass landing of airborne troops on the Downs. Simultaneously, attacks were to be made between Deal and Ramsgate. (Subsequently these plans were extended to project landings in four main areas: from Selsey Bill to Brighton; from Beachy Head to Bexhill; from Cliffs End to Dungeness, and from Dungeness to Folkestone. They were to be accompanied by a heavy aerial bombardment of London.) D-Day was fixed for 15 September.

Meanwhile people watched from their homes as the real Battle of Britain was fought out in the sky overhead. As the Spitfires and Hurricanes broke up the formations of enemy bombers and protective fighters, Clifford Musgrave remembers seeing half a dozen separate fights develop within view of his office in the Royal Pavilion. After the raiders had been dispersed, the British fighters flew back low over the rooftops of the town performing exuberant 'victory rolls'.

As well they might. For the RAF carried the day, inspiring one of Churchill's most memorable quotes. ('Never in the field of human conflict was so much owed by so many to so few.') And as that incredible summer wore on with no sign of the expected invasion, people began to wonder if it might not materialise after all.

It didn't, of course. But in its place came the Blitz. On 14 September

96. A happy group celebrating VJ Day in August 1945. They are standing in East Street and in the background can be seen English's Oyster Bar which is still in business, 40 years on. The soldier on the left with his finger under his chin is aping Shirley Temple's famous pose

97. *These Brighton and Hove Albion footballers in voluminous shorts and with wry expressions are being put through their paces by some ballet dancers in October 1948. The Albion's manager from 1919 until 1948 was Charlie Webb who had scored the winning goal against 1st Division Aston Villa in 1910 and who received the invitation to be Albion's manager while a POW in the First World War. In 1958 Brighton and Hove Albion joined the 2nd Division, whilst 21 years later the team made it to the 1st Division*

Brighton experienced one of its worst air raids of the war. Twenty high explosive bombs were dropped on Kemp Town alone. The Odeon cinema, which was crowded with children, suffered a direct hit. In another raid, the railway works were the target, and a gas main was set on fire in Preston, projecting flames some 300 feet high. Indeed few days passed without an alert of some sort or another. In all, there were 56 serious raids, and though Brighton came off lighter than many other cities, at the end of the war it was assessed that some 5,000 houses had been either damaged or destroyed. For instance, much of the central area now known as Churchill Square was almost razed to the ground. A bomb fell on the Pavilion lawn, and a German aircraft crashed into St Nicholas' churchyard. Yet miraculously few buildings of historic interest came to much harm.

Throughout these difficult years people carried on their normal lives as best they could. The theatres remained open. Concerts were given in the Pavilion. 'Dance away your dumps at the Dome' proclaimed the Dome. But the Swimming Baths at Hove and Roedean School became naval shore establishments. (As a young naval officer, Prince Philip trained in torpedos at Moore's Garage in Russell Square.) Many of the hotels were taken over too. Australian and New Zealand airmen were billeted at the Grand, the Metropole, the Royal Albion and in Lion Mansions. 'No carpets anywhere, you can imagine the noise,' writes Mrs Brenda Santall. 'Once I was invited to dinner at the Old Ship by an RAAF pilot and it was very calm compared to the somewhat frenzied atmosphere elsewhere.'

The Old Ship took the war in its stride. It became a great gathering place, particularly for servicemen, and was always fully booked. Many of the old staff remained in their jobs. Monsieur Monnier, the Swiss chef, and his son kept culinary standards as high as they could, despite the rationing. The Grettons, another father and son team, upheld the smooth service in the restaurant. Miss Court still ran the downstairs bar as she had done for longer than anyone cared to remember. In fact, it was always known simply as 'Courtie's'. Over the years this cosy haunt had acquired something of a club-like atmosphere, with its deep leather armchairs and funny little wooden tub-seats. By common consent, some of the regulars had their own particular chairs (and woe betide the stranger, even in uniform, who sat in one). Courtie always drew the beer direct from the wood, and served it in a jug. She had her favourites, but if she did not take a fancy to you, you might have to wait a long time before you got your drink. For many visiting servicemen—and who knows, perhaps even for Churchill, Montgomery and many of the other bigwigs who came too—the atmosphere of the whole establishment must have stirred nostalgic thoughts of the Old England they were fighting for.

Once Hitler had become involved in Russia, and the danger of an invasion had finally receded, the town began to overflow with soldiers. A large proportion of them were Canadians, and one morning in 1942 there was a tremendous commotion. Says Musgrave: 'Hundreds of planes flew out

98. Street musicians such as this one man band bring a touch of colour to Brighton's busy streets. It was taken in September 1950. Some street musicians became a celebrated part of the local scene and people still remember Marc Antonio with his harp and Alexander with his violin who played together for years. Today the tradition is continued by buskers in Churchill Square

99. An enthusiastic crowd cheers Don Thompson as he wins the London to Brighton walk in September 1960. Known by the nickname of Mighty Mouse he had won Britain's only gold medal in athletics at the Olympics in the 50,000 metres road walk. His victory was enhanced in the public mind when it became known he had acclimatised himself to the expected Roman temperature by training in his own bathroom. Nowadays, the traffic on the London to Brighton road has increased to such an extent that the safety of such road race entrants can no longer be guaranteed

across the coast and aerial battles broke out in all directions. Destroyers were seen steaming towards the French coast, and a convoy of motor-barges travelling down-Channel was bombed, but the raiders were driven off by RAF fighters while anti-aircraft shore batteries put up an intense barrage against the German raiders. It was the morning of the ill-fated raid on Dieppe, and the following day there were to be seen in the streets of Rottingdean and Brighton little groups of haggard Canadian soldiers who had been landed at Newhaven after the raid.'

In due course the GIs appeared in Brighton, and expectations of the second front in Europe grew daily. Behind folds in the Downs and along tree-sheltered lanes, concentrations of tanks, guns and lorries built up steadily. The number of troops in the town increased dramatically. Prominent among the wide array of regimental badges were those of the Welsh Guards, whose officers were to be seen dining, in burnished splendour and apparently carefree hilarity, most evenings at the Old Ship.

One day they did not appear, and the huge military concentrations disappeared too. Then at 2.30 on the morning of 6 June 1944, Brighton residents were awakened by a continuous roar overhead. It was far noisier than anything they had heard before. 'Watchers from windows, from the seafront and the streets saw the dark shapes of the immense fleet of bombers, fighters, transport planes and gliders silhouetted against the moonlit sky as they passed over the coast towards France' recalls our friend Musgrave.

100. Two of the Brighton Tigers in June 1964 looking happy after their team beat Altrincham Aces 22–4 in the Brighton tournament final. The Brighton Tigers were a famous ice hockey team who were British champions three times. Less than a year after this photograph was taken, the Brighton Tigers were no more; the ice stadium in West Street closed down and there was no rink of comparable size for them to use

'Many of them, bombers and fighters, passed and repassed again and again as the morning wore on, and across the water was heard the dull rumble of gunfire and bombing.'

The invasion of Europe had begun. Soon batches of wounded men were being brought into the Brighton hospitals, and German prisoners of war sent off to the local farms to help with the harvest.

Sadly, one of the Welsh Guards' first casualties was Lieutenant Rex Whistler, the brilliant young artist. Not long after the news of his death in action had been received, it was discovered that his last days had been spent painting some remarkable murals in one of the houses where the battalion had been billeted. Almost a complete wall of the officers' mess was covered with a fresco depicting a preposterously gross figure, naked save for the order of the Garter resting on its right buttock, which was kneeling before a recumbent girl with a girdle marked 'Brightelmstone'. A cartouche stated 'Allegory: HRH The Prince Regent awakening the Spirit of Brighton'. This charmingly droll painting, which itself rather touchingly reveals the spirit of a young man on the eve of D-Day, can now be seen in the Royal Pavilion.

When, nine months later, the proclamation of victory had to be read from the Town Hall, the Mayor of Brighton was so small that he could not see over the balcony wall. An elevated platform had to be constructed so that he could catch a glimpse of the people below. But, as the poor chap told his secretary afterwards, he found it difficult to do justice to the occasion. During the whole of his speech he was terrified of falling off into the crowd.

In retrospect, we know that the post-war era which began that day made a clear break with the past. In the new epoch which was starting, could the Brighton of old survive? Obviously not, if some people had their way.

Between councillors who wanted to turn Brighton into a day trippers' paradise (like Blackpool?) and conservationists who sought to retain its Georgian elegance, the rivalry was intense. And some preposterous sugges-

101. Not surprisingly this appealing face captured a great deal of attention. It belonged to a six-month-old seal pup washed up on Shoreham beach in January 1969. She was covered in oil (which took three days to clean off) and was cut and bruised from the stones on the beach. She was taken to the Aquarium and nursed back to health while hundreds of letters poured in enquiring after her. She was named 'Sunshine' and stayed at the Aquarium to become a firm favourite with the crowds

102. As every beachcomber realises—you never know what might be washed up. In January 1980, a 3,500 ton Greek cargo vessel called Athina B grounded on the beach east of the Palace Pier and opposite to Madeira Drive. The Shoreham lifeboat rescued all 21 people on board in dreadful weather conditions. The Athina B caught the popular imagination and hordes of people from all over the country came to Brighton to view the wreck. Sea-front shops and cafés did a roaring trade. When she was refloated in February 1980, about 30,000 people lined the shore to say good-bye as Athina B slipped away into the mist and a Salvation Army band played Rule Britannia

tions were put forward. One aimed at creating a 'Coney Island' type of funfair on the sea-front. Another proposed to clear away the Regency buildings facing the sea and replace them with modern blocks of flats modelled on that architectural sore thumb known as Embassy Court. Equally monstrous was the proposal to bulldoze the Lanes.

But for calculated vandalism nothing could beat the Hove Town Council's decision to demolish two of the most famous groupings of Regency-style houses, Brunswick Square and Adelaide Crescent—which miraculously had emerged unscathed by the war—and build skyscraper blocks in their place (with central car parks instead of the gardens). But luckily a

storm of protests greeted this decision. The national press was up in arms. There was a leader in *The Times*. As a result, the decision was overruled, and no more was heard of this outrageous plan. But a positive outcome of the fuss was the formation of the Regency Society, which has assiduously safeguarded the local Georgian heritage ever since.

Looking back, one realises what a splendid job the local authorities have done in reconciling the antagonistic demands of the We's and the They's. It cannot have been easy, for feelings ran high.

There are moments of recollection. Forty years later, I can see myself driving along the front (the ghost of that undergraduate at Magdalen, unaware that he's being watched by me now, a stranger old enough to be his father) and parking my little MG among the Alvises and Bentleys outside the Old Ship. Was it painted white in those days, or a very pale cream? Inside the ambience was one of polished oak panelling. In the bar to the right, the first person I came across was my bank manager, accompanied by a lady who was clearly not his wife. (Mutual embarrassment, insincere offers of drinks.) Having called on him in his office at Oxford only the previous day, I couldn't help wondering how, so incongruously appearing in a loud check suit with a dazzling tootsie on his arm, he had managed to dodge the head receptionist, a spinster lady whose eagle eyes were known to sort out any dubious 'Mr & Mrs Smiths' at once. If Brighton was notorious for dirty

103. John Richards, general manager, greets HRH Princess Alexandra at the Old Ship, 7 September 1983

159

week-ends, she made sure that there was none of that sort of thing at the Old Ship. She had been doing it for at least 50 years. (But perhaps they were not staying in the hotel?).

Tactfully disentangling myself, I slipped downstairs to where Courtie was still, well yes, holding court. It was here, John Bacon tells me, that many of the most influential people, both in and out of the Town's council, met for a chat. Men such as Antony Dale, Sir William Teeling, D. L. Murray, Eric Gillett, J. L. Denman, Clifford Musgrave and even Sir John Betjeman, conservationists. Lewis (Lord) Cohen with his ambitious scheme to build a huge entertainment pavilion between West Street and Little Russell Street. Tom Arnold with his spectacular ice-shows at S.S. Brighton. H. F. Brazenor of the Dome, Roy Badley who was restoring the Royal Pavilion. E. J. Hutchins, William Stone, and S. M. Caffyn, with their hopes of establishing a university in Stanmer Park. Any of these men who helped shape the destiny of the town may have been there that Saturday morning. A pity I couldn't identify them. All the same, it is pleasant to reflect how much of Brighton's recent history and progress have stemmed from the discussions they had—each in his own chair, or place at the bar—and the decisions that were taken at 'Courtie's'.[2]

2. George Scatliffe, now a consultant with solicitors Donne, Mileham & Haddock, writes: 'I first became acquainted with this friendly hostelry in the early 1930s when as a law student I became Hon. Sec. to the Necessity Club which had its headquarters downstairs in Courtie's Bar. The club was called that because it consisted of young lawyers, barristers and solicitors, and its motto was "necessitas non habet leges". After pre-prandial drinks in Courtie's bar the members, usually a dozen or more, would repair to the music room adjoining on the east side for dinner, so well organised by the then manager Mr Hindle or Mr Greenwood, his assistant. The deputy head waiter assigned to us a splendid man, Emile. A Pin (5 gallons) could be had for something like £3 and I well remember organising a mock trial in fancy dress at which the Registrar of the Brighton County Court, Sir Arthur Jennings, sat in judgement in a defended paternity suit. Hugh Somers-Clarke (of Howlett & Clarke) dressed with a plume in his wide brimmed hat as mother of the dishonoured girl. The plume consisted of a sprig of Pampas grass, and I shall never forget the sight of Sir Arthur rocking with laughter as Bruce Dutton Briant (later Brighton County Court Judge) struck a match and set light to the Pampas grass . . .'

CHAPTER 15

The Offbeat Years

gay tasty loud blowy red gold hopping tingling jellied sand boat pier bunting
candyfloss fish sport cats transistor crash guitar birds kite dance roundabout eels
scene huge new mellow happy lazy high blue green cool spring sun sea music
cloud orchestra pavilion terrace theatre cake art symphony diver steak show dogs
poetry happening
(*Permutation Poem*, written by Edwin Morgan for the Brighton Festival 1967)

104. Sunshine and sea and striped deck-chairs—a perennial Brighton scene. This part of the sea-front from the Old Ship to West Street has changed little over the years and indeed is the core of old Brighton with the famous Lanes not many minutes walk away

Forty years later, Brighton still seemed to be marvellously unchanged. In
the space of just half a life-time—surely one of the fastest evolving periods
in mankind's story—so many other places had become almost unrecognis-
able. As the pastoral world retreats before the assaults of our material
civilisation, one looks back with regret at those elegiac Tuscan villages and
Alpine resorts that have now become suburbs; and who can not feel wistful
at the thought of London itself, where the well-mannered elegance of one's
youthful haunts has dissolved beneath the inexorable pressures of progress
and taxation, to say nothing of traffic?

But at first glance Brighton appeared hardly to have altered at all. Across
from the Old Ship were the same pebbly beach and familiar piers (even if
West Pier was dejectedly boarded up). At the corner of Ship Street was the
fish and chips shop above which Winston Churchill had lodged as a boy;
beyond it the little sweet shops that still sold sticks of rock and the tastiest
of barley-sugar. Cheery crowds still promenaded along the Front; recumbent figures in deck-chairs read their papers; buskers busked and children
frolicked. The contrasting profiles of the Grand (still unbombed) and the

Metropole projected an aura of Edwardian grandeur, while behind its spacious lawns the resplendent panorama of Hove was as handsome as ever, unvulgarised by bombast.

Yet once one's eyesight became adjusted, it became apparent that this sense of immutability, this stasis, was illusive. Like a mirage in the morning, it concealed the fact that, in its incorrigibly individualist way, Brighton had not only kept up with the times but was energetically poised to leap into the future. With remarkable prescience, the borough had grown into an industrial complex, a university town, a conference centre, while at the same time blossoming out as an international tourist resort. And the more one thought about it, the more one realised what master-strokes of unobtrusive planning lay behind these conflicting achievements.

The visual aspect, for instance. Clearly it was imperative that the Georgian heritage should not be dwarfed by indiscriminate building. So the principle was established that the façade from Black Rock to the Aquarium should be protected, and that high buildings erected between the piers must be away from the sea-front and progressively diminish in size to be in scale with Brunswick Terrace.

When, to allay public anxiety over such future building, Sir Hugh Casson was called in by the Corporation to advise them on planning the centre of Brighton, he immediately recommended that the Lanes should be revitalised as a shopping precinct. After all, the higgledy-piggledy network of flint-walled alleys, where the pungency of the past really seemed to linger, formed the kernel of the old town: Brighton's Kasbah, he called it. And so in due course Brighton Square, with its mesh of boutiques and open-air cafés, emerged to become one of the most festive and picturesque places in town (and incidentally, the top tourist draw). Equally felicitous was the creation of a similar shopping precinct known as Duke's Lane, on the site of a large garage between Ship Street and Middle Street.

However, as a muscular foil to these frivolous delights, the Churchill Square development fell like a pile of cement hardly more than a stone's throw away. Stretching from Western Road to the sea-front, this huge shopping complex with its spacious tiled piazzas, its steel and glass super-markets, its office blocks and its multi-storey car park must be, I suppose, the mid-twentieth century's most macroscopic artifact in these parts, uncompromisingly pointing the way to conspicuous consumption (and reminding one that Brighton is now one of the most convenient places in which to shop). No wonder that the gigantic piece of abstract sculpture slap in the centre was, without a hint of irony, called 'The Spirit of Brighton'. As you pause in your window shopping to survey this concrete monstrosity, you realise that for all its Georgian elegance the boisterous old town is fully in tune with the times, even if it slyly hustles changes through the service door.

Though S.S. Brighton of blessed memory had little architectural merit either, the Entertainment Centre that replaced it looks more like a prison than a pleasure dome. (Sadly West Street, with its garish pin-table par-lours, is now squalid enough to turn Mrs Thrale or Dr Johnson in their venerable graves.) But for good or for ill, such things are part of the present-day ethos—as are the massive expense-account conventions which Brighton, like a perfect host or madam, has sought to tempt in its direction by providing something for everyone. So it comes as no surprise to find that the new Conference Centre is the largest in Britain.

At first conventions were held in the Dome (with unconscious humour, since it was built to house horses) or in the Metropole Hotel's Exhibitions Centre. But once such foregatherings had become big business, a great new building was put up on the sea-front. The Brighton Centre was designed to outrival any other place in the country. And indeed with accommodation for nearly 6,000 delegates, simultaneous translation equipment, TV facilities and all the rest, it thrust Brighton firmly into the top international league: a potential rival, maybe, to Venice or Cannes.

Since the seventies the annual Political Conferences have been held here, alternating with Blackpool. And while most Party bigwigs commandeer suites in the Metropole, the Grand or the Bedford, some discriminating politicians prefer to take refuge in the club-like atmosphere of the Old Ship. Denis Healey, for one, always makes it his headquarters. 'I must get back to the Old Ship for a good night's sleep' were his parting words in one radio interview.

When the deputy leadership of the Labour Party was being decided between himself and Tony Benn, both candidates were staying in the hotel. I forget which member of the staff it was who told me that when the ballot came out in his favour, Denis Healey gave a champagne party to celebrate his victory. As the corks were popping, his discomforted opponent turned up and crossly refused to join him for a drink. Instead, Tony Benn made great play of striding over to the fish and chips shop for a meal. Needless to say the media lapped this up. But once the TV cameras had done their stuff, it was remarkable how quickly he returned to the hotel for his dinner.

If there is a touch of political orneriness about this slightly unkind little story, the staff all agree that while Conservative delegates are inclined to be tight-fisted, Labour supporters are noticeably open-handed with their money. But the biggest spenders of all are TUC officials, who lash out with gusto. And at breakfast one morning I remember watching some members boisterously downing champagne (non-vintage, one hopes) with their kippers and scrambled eggs in the best Regency manner, though with rather less style. Manners maketh man, perhaps, but history maketh manners.

The saddest and most dramatic episode in these political foregatherings occurred during the Conservative Party Conference in October 1984, when the IRA planted a bomb in the Grand Hotel with the intention of assassinating the Prime Minister and leading members of her Cabinet. Everyone knows how it exploded at 3 a.m., ripping out a huge section of the upper floors and killing or maiming a number of notable people. Fortunately, the main impact of the blast went upwards rather than downwards, otherwise the death toll might have been considerably worse. As it was, the centre of the hotel was practically gutted, and the Prime Minister's bathroom, which she had vacated only moments before while working on her Conference speech in the adjoining sitting room, was completely destroyed. The Home Secretary and other cabinet ministers had equally lucky escapes, though Norman Tebbit and his wife, who occupied a suite above, were seriously hurt.

John Richards immediately placed the chairman's suite in the Old Ship at Mrs Thatcher's disposal, but for safety reasons the police preferred to take her to the security of the police station. And punctually at nine o'clock, with not a hair out of place, she made her entrance on to the Party rostrum as if nothing had happened. Talk of an Iron Lady!

Curiously, if there was one person in the whole wide world who didn't speedily hear of the disaster, it was the *Washington Post* correspondent at the Conference. Although staying at the Old Ship only a few hundred yards up the road, he slept right through the bombing and was having a late breakfast in his room when the telephone rang. 'Don't you think it's time you filed something about the bomb?' came the voice of his news editor, some 4,000 miles away.

'What bomb?' asked the correspondent, spluttering into his bacon and eggs.

Apart from the conferences, Brighton's theatrical tradition stimulated the organisation of numerous festivals and fairs. The town was chosen to form part of the Festival of Britain in 1951, and the year before that its own Centenary Festival was held to commemorate the purchase of the Royal Pavilion. An event, it should be added, which very nearly never happened at all.

The fact is that once Queen Victoria had gutted the Pavilion of its furniture and fittings, Parliament debated a bill authorising the government to sell or demolish the building. It was no secret that Cubitt's were negotiating to put up rows of houses on the site.

But so strong was local feeling at the prospect of losing the Pavilion, so vocal the protests, that the Commons agreed to give the town a chance to purchase the property for the sum of £53,000 (a bargain when you think that it cost the Prince Regent seven times that amount). The Town Commissioners accepted this attractive offer. However, as so often happens, they had hardly done so than there was a backlash of opposition to the purchase. To a large extent this was prompted by personal animosity against their Clerk, Lewis Slight, who was the driving force behind the resolution to acquire the Pavilion. Jealous critics believed he had the Commission under his thumb. 'The King of Brighton', they called him. So a motion was tabled to rescind the agreement.

At this point Slight lived up to his nickname. After several hours of acrimonious debate, when it looked as if the motion would be carried, he blandly announced that the discussion was unnecessary, since he had been up to London the previous day and already signed the contract. He then outmanoeuvred his infuriated opponents by arranging for a public poll to be held—and scraped through with a majority of just 36 votes.

That was in December 1849. A hundred years later, Slight's high-handed action was celebrated by carrying out a complete restoration of the Pavilion holding a series of Regency exhibitions. Queen Elizabeth II contributed to their success by lending a number of items that George IV had originally bought for the Pavilion, and these were complemented by loans of silver and gold plate from Earl Spencer and the Marquess of Londonderry.

By the sixties, festivals were becoming an everyday feature of the Brighton scene. The first International Festival of the Arts was held. Son et Lumière performances were given in the grounds of the Royal Pavilion. A

Sussex-Normandy Fair ('Ooh-la-la in the Lanes' commented the press, 'a touch of French dressing for Brighton') was so successful that it was followed up by a nine-day Gastronomic Festival. By the time the Brighton Festival was staged in 1967, with an impressive programme of theatrical and musical events, to say nothing of items such as 'environmental sculpture' on the Regency Square lawn and 'concrete poetry' which was displayed around the town and on the buses,[1] it must have seemed to many visitors that Brighton was perpetually en fête. Teenagers dancing through the night to the sound of a dozen rival pop groups—'The Who' made their début here on Brighton front—and huge pylons bearing the words 'Love', 'Beauty', 'Passion' that bobbed about on anchored rafts out at sea until they drooped into the water (all passion bent, a voice was heard to say): all this contributed to give the impression that the town itself had become delightfully off-beat too.

Clearly it was now a place of youth, of life, of love, of laughter. But unhappily it was also a place of violence and drugs. The first cult group to hit Brighton in these postwar years were the teddy-boys of the Fifties. Dressed in knee-length black jackets, drainpipe trousers and bootlace ties, their pimply faces made these mock-Edwardian clothes look all the more absurd. Hence the hostility they aroused, which led to fisticuffs in the local cinemas and dance halls. Most of them carried flick-knives, and when a number of innocent bystanders were slashed in the scuffles, groups of truculent teds were escorted to the railway station and put on the next train home by the police.

Their successors were the beatniks—or beachniks as they were known—whose contempt for society was expressed in a fondness for dirt and LSD. Their personal revolt against material values took the shape of verminous clothes and sharing food or sex in common. Men and women alike wore ragged jeans and army-disposal coats; they did little more than sit listlessly around on the pebbles, occasionally stirring themselves to take dips in the sea while still fully dressed. 'The not uncommon spectacle of a young girl, ragged dirty and barefoot, with tangled lice-infected hair, who could have been beautiful, and whose pleasant voice proclaimed her gentle upbringing, but in whose face one seemed to detect a deep unhappiness, was a disturbing experience' commented a kindly observer. But after a season or two the authorities decided to discourage these drug-addicted vagrants from sleeping on the beach by washing it down with hoses in the middle of the night. Whereupon the beachniks departed to join their fellow devotees in Tangiers or Nepal.

The swinging Sixties brought visitors of a different sort. Suddenly the world of youth was divided into Rockers and Mods, who screamed into Brighton like hordes of lemmings on their motor bikes and scooters.

In contrast to the beachniks, Mods were modishly hooked on clothes. They sported the latest Carnaby Street confections and favoured Vespas or Lambrettas because a scooter was unlikely to soil their elegant get-ups. Though for the most part junior clerks and shop assistants or simply living on the dole, they managed to become the new fashion-spenders and trend setters. Apart from clothes, they were addicted to pop music and pep-pills.

---

1. A sample is given at the head of this chapter.

105. The heyday of the Mods and Rockers. Taken in May 1964 this photograph shows the deck chair battle in progress on the Sun Terrace of the Aquarium. At the height of the disturbance the crowd numbered between 2,000 to 3,000

Cut now, as they say in filmland, to black. The Rockers were working-class toughs who swaggered about in black leather jackets adorned with brass studs and chains, and rode powerful Harley-Davidson or BMW bikes, if not some early kamikase devices from Japan. They regarded the Mods as cissies, and went for them whenever they had chance to do so without being outnumbered (for there were many fewer Rockers than Mods).

Fights flared up between the two groups at Clacton and Hastings, but nothing like the battle that took place on the front at Brighton during the Whitsun weekend in 1964. It resulted in a good deal of damage and a number of people being injured. Was the rumour true that money had changed hands so that the press could get some pictures of teen-age violence? Who knows. However, some stiff sentences were slapped on the offenders for carrying offensive weapons and assaulting the police.

After this, the Mod craze seemed to run out of steam. But perhaps this was because its addiction to hard rock, indiscriminate sex and hallucinating 'highs' had become part of teen-age life. Granted, the convention of unconventionality now decreed androgenous jeans and longer hair for the boys than the girls (which at least had the merit of concealing many villainous faces). And for a while the Flower Children provided some diversion with their disarming slogan 'make love not war'. But so far as Brighton was concerned, the new University of Sussex was taking over as the focus of youthful activities.

An intellectual nerve-centre! Hardly the image that this town normally brings to mind. But the idea of establishing a university had been aired as early as 1911. Preference was given to developing the Polytechnic. But then, just a century after its acquisition of the Royal Pavilion, the Borough brought off another far-sighted coup by purchasing Stanmer Park, formerly the seat of the Earls of Chichester. And it soon became apparent that this beautiful estate, so conveniently situated on the Downs near the village of

106. The interdenominational Meeting House at the University of Sussex. The photograph was taken in 1967 and also shows the fine wooded setting of the campus

Falmer, was the perfect location for a new university.

This was the first of seven so-called 'plate-glass' universities to be founded in Britain at the beginning of the Sixties. Architecturally speaking, of course, the University of Sussex is constructed more of brick and prefabricated concrete than of glass: it consists of a complex of buildings radiating from Falmer House with its large central courtyard. The dining hall rises through two storeys to a barrel-vaulted roof; but though the inside of the staircase tower is lined with squared flints in the Sussex idiom, and the circular meeting house with its lop-sided roof was clearly inspired by an oast-house, the only visible link with the past (across a fold in the Downs) is Stanmer House itself, which served for a time as the university's administrative headquarters. In the early eighteenth century the grounds were gracefully landscaped round the Pelhams' Palladian mansion, and Sir Basil Spence cleverly fitted the buildings into the scenery, so that hardly a tree was disturbed.

The new foundation attracted some fine academic talent, which combined with the student body to give the place a radical, laid-back atmosphere. In 1963 Sussex received its Royal charter along with a coat of arms from the College of Heralds. It also acquired such an immediate reputation for militant dissent that any local display of ungodliness, permissiveness or political intransigence was immediately attributed to 'the wise non-virgins of Sussex University'. A national newspaper complained that it had become 'a place of drugs and debauchery, sin and sensuality'. Questions about it were even raised in Parliament.

If one smiles at the notion of wordly old Brighton being corrupted by its students, there is little doubt that the advent of such a large body of exuberant young people livened things up. For landladies, of course, it was a windfall. The newcomers gave them the chance to charge summer rates in the depth of off-season. Those undergraduates not living on campus lodged in boarding houses around the town; their rooms became redolent with Trotskyist theories and the sweet smell of hash. It may well be that in the aggregate they helped to turn this Tory stronghold into a Labour seat (by a margin of 7 votes) in the General Election of 1964. (Incidentally, at the moment of writing there are 4,300 students and a staff of about 2,000 at Sussex University; also 7,500 students attending the Brighton Polytechnic, if you include 2,000 part-timers—and the Brighton seats are once again Tory!) But this young blood also added flare and zing to the place, while the permanent teaching staff provided an academic infusion to cultural movements of both advocacy and protest. Above all the educational thrust contributed to the development of Brighton as a truly international resort by making it one of the chief language-teaching centres in the country. Walking through Brighton's streets, you can hear every possible language being spoken, but Brighton's tuition will enable a Chinese from Hong Kong, say, to discuss fertiliser manufacturing with an Arab from the Emirates.

And help them with their technical problems too, if my friends at Ewbank Preece are brought into the action. For Brighton is now a nerve-centre not only of cultural and technical education, but also of expertise in commerce and industry. There was a time when the railway workshops accounted for most of its manufacturing activity, but since the war, factories have appeared and offices opened. Astonishingly enough, Brighton is now a hub of big business.

Granted that it's no Huddersfield or Slough (and just as well, too). But a proliferation of industrial plants have sprung up around Portslade; while Legal & General, the Alliance and Leicester Building Society, and American Express are among the great organisations that have moved their headquarters to Brighton or Hove.

The Alliance is actually a local concern: it started off in 1863 as The Brighton & Sussex Equitable Permanent Benefit Building Society. The total of its loans then amounted to £3,345. Between 1929 and the outbreak of World War II, its assets rose from £20,000 to £4½ million. In 1985, with assets exceeding £1 billion, the Alliance merged with the Leicester, bringing their combined assets to over £6,000 million.

In leafy suburban streets where retired empire-builders once resided, you may now sense the sharpness of high technology. Did not Archimedes declare that if given a place to stand on he would move the earth? Yes, and believe me, from such an unlikely fulcrum one of the largest consulting organisations in Europe is doing just that (allowing, of course, for a touch of poetic licence).

This too is something of a home-grown saga. To elaborate: just a century ago, when electro-dynamics were still in their infancy, a firm called Edmundson's Electricity Corporation was formed to generate and distribute electrical power. And when the industry was nationalised in 1946, Harry Ewbank, who was then its chief engineer, got together with some of his colleagues to form Ewbank & Partners Ltd, consultants in the field of electrical engineering.

Some fifty years previously, Sir William Preece had given up the job of chief engineer at the General Post Office to join his son Arthur and Major Philip Cardew, who was electrical adviser to the Board of Trade, in founding a partnership known as Preece, Cardew & Rider (PCR). Among other activities, they specialised in the embryonic science of telecommunications, and still treasure a letter written to Preece in 1896 introducing 'a young Italian of the name of Marconi, who has come over to this country with the idea of getting taken up a new system of telegraphy without wires at which he has been working'. (It appeared to be based on the use of Herzian waves and Oliver Lodge's coherer, the correspondent explained.)

107. Prince Michael of Kent, President of the R.A.C., driving a 1902 Wolseley, was one of 330 entrants in the London to Brighton Veteran Car Run in November 1984. The Wolseley, which was closely followed by security officers in a Jaguar, broke down twice

In the course of time both of these engineering concerns extended their range of technology to the point where many of their operations were complementary and indeed overlapping. Working concurrently in Brighton, it was clearly to their advantage to pool their resources. So in 1982 they decided to merge. The decision was wise: with a staff of 1,500 located in some forty project offices around the world, Ewbank Preece's activities now encompass the whole spectrum of energy and telecommunications. From their new headquarters in Davigdor Road just out of the centre of the town, they direct a thesaurus of projects ranging from steam turbine plants in New Zealand to microwave radio networks in Papua New Guinea. During the last few years their programme has included a communications control system for the Hong Kong police, a solar power supply in Djibouti, a hydro-electric power station in Pakistan; and they have undertaken projects as diverse as fisheries in Bali and fertiliser manufacturing in Qatar. And some of the undertakings are by no means new. For instance, in 1900 one of their founding figures was retained to design the first public electricity supply system for Sydney in Australia. Over eighty years and some 25,000 MW of commissioned plant later, they are still working for the Sydney County Council. If Puck told the King of the Fairies that he would put a girdle round about the earth in 40 minutes, our friends in Brighton would surely know how to do it in under 40 seconds.

But equally, as the Group Director David Jones (who is also Chairman of the Brighton Polytechnic) reminded me, they have a strong commitment to their home town and its heritage—which is probably why Ewbank bought the Old Ship from John Bacon's family six years ago. It was a prestige project, like the refurbishing of the Cutty Sark and the Ivory Warehouse in London's St Katherine's Wharf, or the restoration of the sixteenth-century Long Gallery roof at Sutton Place. And, by pleasant coincidence, there may be a connection between the inventor of electro-magnetism and the Old Ship Hotel. Michael Faraday rarely travelled far from the Royal Institution

108. *To celebrate the 88th anniversary of the Veteran Car Rally in 1984 this 3½ h.p. Fiat built in 1899 was on display in the foyer of the Old Ship Hotel. The author Raymond Flower talks to Mr John Richards (General Manager) and Major John Bacon (Vice-Chairman) seated in the car*

in London. But he was a close friend of Paganini, and is known to have come to Brighton in December 1831 for a lecture given in the Assembly Rooms on the paper he had just read to the Royal Society on his research into the induction of electric currents. It appears more than likely, therefore, that Faraday not only attended Paganini's concert on 9 December 1831, but also stayed at the hotel immediately after the lecture on his crowning discovery.

So now, under the guiding hand of its general manager, John Richards, the Old Ship is gently being revivified. There may not be much that can be done about the unlovely extension built in 1965 which improved the interior accommodation but hardly embellished the venerable façade. Inside, however, John and his wife Fiona have skilfully redecorated Tettersell's Bar and the main dining room (replacing, thank goodness, the distracting red and black striped leathery wallpaper that had been put up at great cost by a trendy London decorator) and freshened up the bedrooms. Since John graduated from the Savoy and is well versed in the art of good living, it is not surprising that much emphasis is being placed on the cuisine and the cellar. He is admirably backed up by a fine chef, Bernard Schröter, and Monsieur Gilles in the restaurant, who are given full rein to their talents; in fact those with grumpy livers can easily do themselves an injury if they are tempted to indulge too enthusiastically in their culinary skills. (But a brisk walk along the front should soon put matters right.)

At what point, then, does the present stop and the future begin? Already the Brighton of 1946—the clothes and the cars and the smell of Abdullah cigarettes—is difficult to describe in the vocabulary of the Eighties. So it is perfectly impossible to peer forwards for more than a year or two at what lies ahead. Will the Marina—the most elaborate and costly scheme ever conceived for Brighton—become the yachtsman's paradise that Henry Cohen dreamt of, instead of the concrete slum for boats that it is today? Will the new Ramada Hotel and the renovated Queen's and Royal Albion transform that rather grotty nub of Brighton's sea-front into a rival to the Croisette? Will the West Pier really be rebuilt?

It's easy to be a Cassandra. It's also easy to see *la vie en rose*. But somewhere between these two extremes is that funny old British way of just muddling through. And so, as I write these concluding lines, I foresee neither apocalypse nor eldorado. I can't help thinking that a hundred years from now, when today's great grandchildren are off for week-ends round the galaxy, happy earth-bound folk will still be coming down to Brighton for a breath of fresh air and fun.

And doubtless they will echo Sir John Betjeman's comforting words: 'I often stayed at the Old Ship with my father and associate it with cigar smoke and happiness and Volk's electric railway.'

109. One of the 330 entrants in the 1984 London to Brighton Veteran Car Run was Mr Thomas Love of Perth pictured here with his sister Elizabeth in his 1904 Rolls-Royce

Afterword

This book was begun at Memphis, in Egypt. Parts of it were written at my house in Tuscany, at Raffles Hotel in Singapore, at Batu Ferringhi in Penang, and on Legian Beach in the island of Bali. Brighton in Bali! It sounds like a joke. Yet Brighton's fascination dominated my thoughts in these exotic places (like Sir Osbert Sitwell, who wrote about Brighton in Peking) and kept me happily employed for well over a year. I hope this little volume will now have given you pleasure for an hour or two.

I was encouraged to write it by my old friend and fellow author Sir Donald Hawley, the Chairman of Ewbank Preece, who have owned the Old Ship Hotel since 1979, and Major John Bacon, whose family had done so previously for nearly 150 years. So once again I have used the device of revolving local history around an institution that conjures up the spirit of the place (such as the Palace at St Moritz, or Raffles in Singapore). As Sir Harry Preston observed, 'an hotel is a swing door through which the world walks', and though few hotels can justify the treatment, there is no doubt that the *dramatis personae* who fashioned Brighton have been walking into the Old Ship since Tudor days. Hence my belief that it has been a logical reference point from which to look back, in an impressionistic rather than an academic way, at Brighton's vivid past.

I wanted to write a book that was short rather than long but which, backed by evocative illustrations, would convey the gist of each successive period. Thus I have chipped away at each chapter to reduce its length. At the same time, I have tried not to make the story too tight. I did not want it to taste like condensed milk.

110. Not everyone's idea of fun—a dip in the icy sea on Christmas Day 1984. Over 30 people took part in the event which continues a Christmas tradition stretching back over 100 years. Sea bathing in winter is a Brighton entertainment of even longer standing because in 1782 it was recorded that Dr Johnson's friend, Mrs Thrale, and her three daughters, took a swim by moonlight at 6 o'clock on a November morning

I must record a specially warm word of thanks to Judy Middleton, the historian of Hove, who generously placed her monograph on the Old Ship Hotel at my disposal. What's more, she kept the ball rolling in Brighton while I was on the other side of the globe, and got together the collection of pictures, many of them rare, which add a touch of lustre to it all. We had a lot of fun working together. It was also my good fortune to be able to discuss the manuscript with Professor Geoffrey Blainey, the historian, and his wife Ann, the biographer, while they were staying with me in Tuscany. Nothing could have been kinder than the way that Ann Blainey devoted so much of her summer holiday to combing through the text with a benign but critical eye. A word of thanks equally to Lynn Bresler for dotting some i's and crossing a few t's.

Finally, I must thank Roger Reed, the Chairman of the Old Ship Hotel board, and John Richards, the General Manager, who have given me every possible help, and made available the archives and facilities of their establishment—including some comfortable accommodation for much of the time that I was conducting my research. I am most grateful for their hospitality and support.

Raymond Flower

Index